Writing with a View of the Graveyard

Loss, Life, and Unruly Grace

By Ruth E. Hetland

2018

Create Space Press

Dedicated with love to Betty JoAnne Hetland

and Gordon Cecil Hetland

Contents

Introduction

Dear Reader,

I began writing a blog shortly after my mother died in 2011. As I thought about what to call that blog, the title, "Writing with a View of the Graveyard" seemed to fit because through my office window I could see our church cemetery, and in those first months and years after mom died, I saw everything through the lens of loss. Every occasion was something I didn't get to share with her. Each sermon I wrote had her lingering somewhere in the background and became another chance to reflect on grief, loss, death, and resurrection. Whenever the seasons changed, it was another moment to remember what it was like when she was still around to experience them with me. My grief was all-consuming, and there was no way out of it except to write. And so, I wrote.

This book is partly an observation of grief, and I pray it might be a comfort to you in times of loss. However, it has become more than that: it is a prayer, a meditation, a devotional, a confession, a journey through the church year, a celebration of love and life, and a reflection on God's unruly grace which is the thread that holds it, and all of us together.

God be near to you in your life
God be near to you in your loss
God surround you with unruly, beautiful, scandalous grace.
In Jesus name, I pray. Amen.

Ruth E. Hetland

2018

Saint Peter's Lutheran Church
Audubon, Minnesota

Waffles and Coffee

There are countless viewpoints on heaven. Some are cobbled together from what the Bible says about heaven or from stories or movies about near-death experiences. There are some who think we exist in a heaven or hell of our own making right here on earth.

I never spent much time thinking about heaven until my mother died. In the months that followed, every time I went running at night I looked up at the stars and I missed her so completely, my bones ached. I found comfort in imagining Heaven.

In those dreams, Heaven looks like this: I will sit down at my mom's kitchen table and eat waffles that she is making for me on grandma's waffle iron. When she's used up all the batter, and all the golden-brown waffles are all stacked on a plate, she'll sit at the table with me, and we'll drink coffee and eat waffles with peanut butter and syrup. We'll talk, and it will seem as though not a moment has passed since we saw each other. We'll have the blessed ease of just being mother and daughter again – how we were when we were at our best. It won't be how it was when I was a teenager and blaming her for everything that went wrong. It won't be how it was at the end when I was trying to take care of her and so desperate to keep death away. Those memories will still be a part of us for they are a part of our story, but the sting and the pain will be gone. All that will remain is the love and the goodness and the wholeness there was to existence when I had a mom, a friend, so wonderful.

It's been years since mom died. Grief is still my companion, but she doesn't smother me as much these days. She's always around, sometimes just quietly lingering in the background and yet at other times, just when I notice how she's beginning to fade, she'll come and slap my face hard. I'm glad for the tears she brings with her and the ways she twists and hurts my heart. I welcome the darkness she brings to an otherwise beautiful day. Her presence reminds me of the blessing I had for so long. I don't mind Grief tagging along with me for the rest of my days because she helps to fill part of the emptiness in my life that mom left behind. I don't expect or want that empty spot to ever be filled entirely with joy, sweetness, calm or peace again. God is bringing me those things, and I am grateful. However, there's a space reserved for Grief as long as she will stay.

I've been thinking I know something more now than I ever could before about the origin of the deep sighs, eyes that hold the wisdom of the ages, stooped backs, the wakeful hours in the middle of the night, and the color of weary gray. There is so much loss this world holds. Grief needs so much space here so she seeps in where she will. She dries up the creekbeds and starves the crops and steals into every one of our homes to take up residence there. She'll take up as much room as we give her. She can be the queen of everything or a shadow in the corner. Give her too much power, and she'll gladly ruin the rest of your days. Give her a spot in the corner, and she'll be just the reminder you need that life is both beauty and sadness, love and loss. Walk gently. See each other and help each other along the journey. Cry, laugh, be real.

No, I don't mind the Grief. I hope a bit of her always stays. Her presence is what keeps my eyes looking at the stars and dreaming about what is yet to come. She keeps me thinking about the Place where my mother and my grandmothers and friends have already gone and where I hope to join them someday. At the end of this life. Waffles and coffee, conversation at a kitchen table. Home.

> *Don't let this throw you. You trust God, don't you? Trust me. There is plenty of room for you in my Father's home. If that weren't so, would I have told you that I'm on my way to get a room ready for you? And if I'm on my way to get your room ready, I'll come back and get you so you can live where I live. – John 14:2 The Message – MSG*

Prayer: Dear God, thank you for all that I have learned along the way, even the hard, bittersweet, aching lessons that have come from grief. In Jesus' name, I pray. Amen.

Reflect: What images come to mind when you consider Heaven?

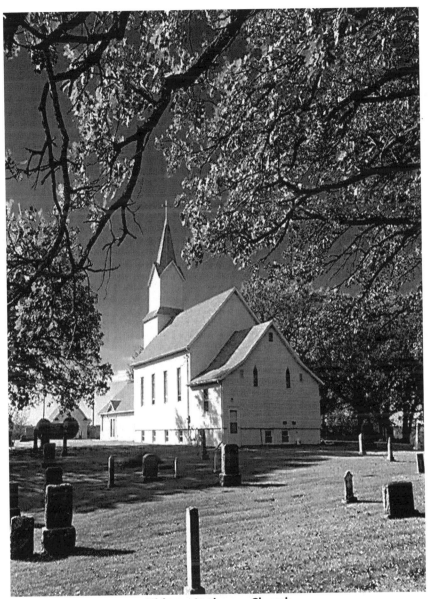

Nidaros Lutheran Church
Clitherall, Minnesota

Emmanuel

In many places, Advent is cold. It is the church season of beginnings, and yet it is winter and dark. There is very little in the natural world pointing toward burgeoning life and yet it is there. Under the ground, the seeds are waiting for the warmth of the sun to bring them to bloom again. The days will be getting longer and warmer again. It may not feel like it will happen soon but the promise of it is there.

And there is a promise for us as well. When we face dead-ends, loss, or weariness, God reminds us:

All will be well. All is yet possible. Don't give up!

No matter how today finds you: whether tired or refreshed, peaceful or anxious, hopeful or hopeless, remember that the story of Advent is the story of Emmanuel, "God with us," and God is always about beginnings. Always. Even in the darkest night. Even in a hospital room. Even in hospice. Because it was even so on the cross.

"Behold, the virgin shall conceive and bear a son, and they shall call his name Emmanuel" (which means, God with us). – Matthew 1:23

Prayer: Dear God, let your joy and hope fill me and flow through me today and help me share that joy and hope with others. In Jesus name, I pray. Amen.

Reflect: Emmanuel means "God with us." Where do you feel God's presence the most? Are there specific times or places you feel closer to God?

Sigdal Lutheran Church
Tolna, North Dakota

Advent

Often during the season of Advent, it is customary to do something to set the season apart to prepare our hearts for Christ's birth. We might collect funds for a cause dear to us, or sometimes churches add a mid-week service in the morning or evening. These rituals help us to pause, reflect and turn our attention toward God in fresh ways.

This year, I gave each family in our church a little cardboard piggy bank to take home for the season of Advent and fill with coins to go toward ELCA World Hunger. I brought our piggy bank home and displayed it prominently on the kitchen table on the first Sunday in Advent. The next day, I found a five-dollar bill in the cemetery and put it in the piggy bank instead of using it to buy myself a latte. Since then, the piggy bank has been sitting unbothered. My plan for putting a little bit of change in there each day mostly forgotten, along with our strategy to light our home advent wreath consistently. Even though I vowed to keep things simple and worry-free this year, I'm already stressing out a little bit about upcoming Christmas services at church and cooking for the extended family on Christmas Day. So far, Advent is quite a bit like every other church season: a season of stops and starts, a time of victories and failures. It turns out that I prepare about as well for the birth of Jesus as I prepare for anything, kind of last minute and haphazard.

It is an imperfect Advent, an imperfect life. That's ok because I take comfort in this: there is some One greater at work in my life than me. We don't often understand how or why life unfolds as it does, and yet there are times we catch glimpses of the beauty and blessedness of it all.

Maybe that will happen to you sometime this Advent season; maybe it won't. Maybe Christmas morning will dawn with fresh peace and renewed strength in your heart, or perhaps you'll wake up with the stomach flu and stay in bed all day. Either way, all is well, because this story we live is about more than you and me, what we do or don't do. It is about God's story. We are part of it, and it is an immense gift. Our most significant task appears to be that we must open our eyes and see it.

Most afternoons this Advent I spend a little time sitting with a parishioner who is now in Hospice care. His remaining time on earth is short. I don't know if he hears me anymore when I read the scripture to him but I still read it, and I pray out loud for him. It seems like a haunting contradiction to walk past the festive lights adorning the hallways of the nursing home to go into his quiet room where death is drawing near. It strikes me that it is precisely in these moments of stark contrasts we often sense the Spirit's presence more closely than ever.

Sitting in that room next to Earl and listening to him breathe with the sounds of the world going on outside has become what will set this Advent apart for me as blessed. It wasn't the ritual I planned or expected, but in it, I have felt God's presence.

11 For surely I know the plans I have for you, says the Lord, plans for your welfare and not for harm, to give you a future with hope. – Jeremiah 29:11

Dear God, thank you for all the surprising ways you find me and hold me near. Amen.

Reflect: When was the last time something turned out very differently than you planned? What was good about it? What was difficult?

Atlanta Lutheran Church
Ulen, Minnesota

Joe

I was not surprised when I heard that Joe's heart stopped beating. We all knew his heart beat in time with Audrey's heart and when she died a few months earlier, it seemed so had the spark of his own life. He spent the last few months journeying through the motions of his days. He sat in church as usual, but without her by his side he always looked a bit lost. He welcomed us into his home to sing Christmas carols, but he didn't try to hold back the tears as we did so. Everything reminded him of her.

When I went to visit Joe in the months after Audrey died, I told him how when I lost my mom it helped to write down my thoughts about her. Joe was raised to believe his pastors had wisdom and so he listened to me. He poured his time and tears into writing down their love story. With his failing eyesight, he recorded the treasured sum of his days with her – his words spoke of true love, pure and sweet, a dear and happy marriage of sixty years.

Joe had always known Audrey was the one. Joe told his friend, Earl, that he was going to marry Audrey shortly before he even asked her out on their first date. It turned out Audrey was fond of Joe, too. She liked his easy smile and soft laugh, and sure enough, by September of that year they were married.

What followed was a good life made beautiful by two people who knew how to be thankful for all they had, to see the blessings all around them, and to pour out generosity and positivity to all who knew them.

I was Joe and Audrey's pastor the five years I was in Texas. I visited Audrey in the hospital and at home many times as her health failed. I presided at her funeral in which her grandchildren sang beautiful songs to honor her memory. My sons and I visited her grave, and my boys picked wildflowers to adorn her resting place.

I moved away to a new call at a church in Minnesota shortly before Joe died. He had been hospitalized with a heart condition, and I came to see him in the hospital up until it was time for the moving van to arrive. The last time I spoke with Joe, it was right before he had a major surgery. I told him I loved him and I would see him later. I meant after the surgery was over, but he never woke up again while I was still in Texas.

On the day of Joe's funeral, just weeks after I left Texas and only days after I started my new call in Minnesota, some other pastor commended Joe to God's care and keeping. It was not me who gathered with this family I grew to love and reminded them of God's eternal promises.

Nobody tells you when you become a pastor how your heart will break for your congregation. Nobody tells you how you will love them like family and no matter how much you might like to treat your work like it is just a job, it is never just a job.

A pastor leaves pieces of her heart with every congregation she serves.

I thank my God for you every time I remember you. Philippians 1:3

Prayer: Dear God, thank you for the blessing of relationships that mean so much to me. In Jesus name, I pray. Amen.

Reflect: When have you had to say a difficult "goodbye?" What helped you and brought you comfort during that time?

Our Savior's Lutheran Church at Norse
Clifton, Texas

Hey Jealousy

We sat at lunch, two friends who had not seen each other for a long time. Out of the blue, she sent an e-mail the week before: "Thinking of you today." I responded with a short note, the kind of note that feels like way too little when you haven't had a proper conversation for nearly a decade. As I closed the note, I wrote, "Do you ever come to Minnesota?" Within a few minutes, she wrote back and said that she was going to be in Minnesota the next week! I checked my schedule and decided that with a little maneuvering, I could make the time to drive the few hours it would take to get to where she would be.

And that is how we came to be sitting at the Riverside Bar in Minneapolis on a sunny November afternoon.

Part of the way through our lunch, she was telling me a story about a recent visit to New York with her husband. He took her to the Cartier store to buy her a present for their tenth wedding anniversary and to celebrate some recent, significant success in their business. She showed me the watch, and it was lovely. The way she phrased the story and talked about the gift, I knew it must have cost a substantial amount. Later that night, curious as to how much it was, I decided to look up how much a Cartier watch costs.

It quite literally took my breath away to think of having a watch that costs that much.

I get judgmental very quickly when I find out people have spent what I perceive to be an excessive amount of money on anything non-essential. I immediately start picturing starving children, homeless families, and all the help that money could have provided. It's not fair that I do this. Someone could look at my overstuffed bookshelves and say, "what a waste – she doesn't need all those."

But it wasn't just my judgmental attitude that I noticed. What surprised me was that when I saw the price tag of a watch like that, I felt the sting of hot tears beginning at the corners of my eyes. I could never afford that watch unless I didn't want my family to eat or pay our bills for a couple of months. In that split second, I felt shabby and ashamed. I was right back in junior high when I had to alternate between wearing my same two pairs of jeans day after day and looked with jealousy at the pretty clothes the other girls had.

It wasn't that I wanted that watch. In fact, I can think of few material things I could want less than an expensive watch. So, I was puzzled at my reaction to it.

It reminded me of when I lived in Texas, and there was a parade of homes each year at Christmas time. I went on the tour one year and vowed never to go again because, with each spectacular house I visited, my own house began to seem smaller and dingier. Before that tour I was satisfied with my warm, cute home, but afterward, for the rest of that day at least, all I could think about was what a bummer it was that other people had so much and I had so little.

The tenth commandment reads: *"You shall not covet anything that belongs to your neighbor."* When we covet, we take our eyes off all that God has given us and instead focus on what other people have. When we do that, it is so easy to start feeling jealous and put-out.

On a typical day, I feel like my world is full of abundance. I marvel at my pretty house, our full refrigerator, our two cars that work great! I lack nothing, and I don't want to forget that. So, it startled me that a gift my friend received should ever bring up a negative feeling in me.

But any of us are capable jealousy or greed or selfishness. No one is immune.

So, what is an efficient way to combat that coveting impulse?

Here is a surefire antidote: give thanks. When I feel jealousy tapping on my shoulder, I make long lists in my mind of all the beautiful things this life has given me, and then I remember there is nothing shabby about me or my days or the space I take up in this world. It isn't possible to focus on gratitude and be jealous at the same time.

A genuinely vibrant and prosperous life can't be purchased at any price. And when I think of my friend's smile as she showed me that watch, I suspect that her joy wasn't in that piece of metal so much as all it represents: a gift from her beloved husband, love and time together, hard work, deep affection, and a significant wedding anniversary. Priceless.

6-7 Don't fret or worry. Instead of worrying, pray. Let petitions and praises shape your worries into prayers, letting God know your concerns. Before you know it, a sense of God's wholeness, everything coming together for good, will come and settle you down. It's wonderful what happens when Christ displaces worry at the center of your life. – Philippians 4:6-7 The Message (MSG)

Prayer: Dear God, let my thoughts and my words overflow with gratitude. In Jesus name, I pray. Amen.

Reflect: What is your "top ten list" of things for which you are thankful?

Hegland Lutheran Church
Hawley, Minnesota

Mary

"And Mary said, yes, I see it all now:
I'm the Lord's maid, ready to serve.
Let it be with me just as you say." (Luke 1:35)

I've been thinking about you, Mary. This time of year, I tend to think of you frequently. This was especially true the two Decembers I was pregnant with my sons. I experienced the Advent season of waiting and expectation in a whole new way then. During the worship services on Christmas Eve those years I was boiling in my clergy robe and stole. My boys were like little furnaces growing bigger by the day. The Christmas tree in the sanctuary at my church in Colorado obstructed the congregation's view of the chairs where the pastors sat, and so during the hymns, I took off my shoes, and rested my face on the cool marble pillar back there. I was so hot, so tired, so not glowing or any of the good things they say about pregnant women. And I thought about you, Mary. You were no longer just a character in a story I had heard my whole life. You were a mom, like me.

But of course, you were much different than me, too, because your pregnancy was announced to you by an angel and all. And you were probably about fourteen years old at most.

So, when Luke writes that you were "perplexed" or "troubled" at what the angel was announcing to you, I tend to think that is an understatement of 'biblical' proportions. I feel perplexed, or a bit troubled when the dryer quits working or if there is a new stain on the couch for which no one is taking responsibility. But when an angel appears with news that is not only going to change your life but the entire world through you, well, I can think of better words to use: stupefied, astonished, flabbergasted, dumbfounded. Uff da.

And, Mary, do you know how streamlined Luke makes your story? Just a few neat and tidy verses and your tale is told. In verse 31 you begin to find out all that is about to happen. You ask one question in verse 34: "how exactly is this going to happen?" and by verse 38 you say, "Okay then, let's do this."

I'm pretty sure that moment wasn't quite so neat, tidy, and quick as Luke portrays it. Mary, only you and God and perhaps Gabriel got a glimpse of how this went down. I've been wondering if you felt terrified, or if you wanted to say, "pick another girl from the village, please!", if you had sleepless nights over the months that followed as you wondered, and worried at this strange blessing happening to you.

You are often portrayed as meek and mild but that's not how I think of you. I think of how brave you were to say, "Here I am, the servant of the Lord, let it be with me according to your word," even if your voice was trembling when you said it. God blessed you with that bravery and Gabriel reminded you that nothing is impossible with God. I wonder if you repeated that to yourself over and over, a mantra of sorts that held you up through the morning sickness, the swelling, the heartburn, all the glorious accompaniments to pregnancy? *"nothing is impossible, nothing is impossible, nothing is impossible with God."*

I think about you, Mary, and this story of how you believed and trusted God. For however many doubts were woven in along with it, God blessed you with just enough faith and you leaned into that faith to carry you through all that was to come. Day by day.

I wish Luke would have written more about you because we are left to wonder so much. If we aren't careful, we can think that you had some superhuman faith and bravery and if we were only better people, we would have that kind of faith and bravery, too. We can think that as followers of God we can't have doubts and we need to be sure and certain all the time.

But you were a fourteen-year-old girl, Mary, maybe as young as twelve. You were the age of a middle-schooler. You were a human being, like any of us. Luke doesn't write about your fears or hesitations; he doesn't linger over how common you were, how utterly unremarkable you were compared to any other girl alive in those days. Instead, he focuses on what happened through you, which is, of course, the point. Jesus is the point. Jesus is the reason. Jesus is Christmas.

But you mattered, Mary. You mattered so much. I hope you knew that. You matter because we all matter. You matter because you remind us that God is able to work through any of us. You remind us that the extraordinary can still happen because nothing is impossible with God.

26-28 In the sixth month of Elizabeth's pregnancy, God sent the angel Gabriel to the Galilean village of Nazareth to a virgin engaged to be married to a man descended from David. His name was Joseph, and the virgin's name, Mary. Upon entering, Gabriel greeted her: Good morning! You're beautiful with God's beauty, beautiful inside and out! God be with you.
29-33 She was thoroughly shaken, wondering what was behind a greeting like that. But the angel assured her, "Mary, you have nothing to fear. God has a surprise for you: You will become pregnant and give birth to a son and call his name Jesus.
(Luke 1: 26-33)

Prayer: Dear God, help me to believe in all that is yet possible in me and through me, by Your grace. In Jesus name, I pray. Amen.

Reflect: Can you think of a Bible story you have heard differently over time as your life experiences and understanding grew?

Leaf Mountain Lutheran Church
Clitherall, Minnesota
(Layered with photo of local trees)

Strong Enough

We're always letting go of something.

Children let go of their youth bit by bit until one day you are teaching them to drive.

We let go of relationships, some more easily and graciously than others.

We let go of ideas of who we thought we might become and live into who we are – this can be both humbling and exhilarating.

We let go of pastimes that no longer serve us as we realize life is precious and short and why hold on to doing certain things if it is just because society or tradition expects it of us?

We let go of perfectionism as we realize our creativity and output can be greater if we don't treat every word, every creation as if it is precious beyond measure. Let it go and let it affect the world. Stop revising.

Sometimes I think learning to let go is one of the greatest lessons of life and I wonder why it can be so hard to do.

I used to have a pair of bold black leather boots with tall, audacious heels. I loved those boots – they made every outfit have just the tiniest bit of edge to it. I might be a mild-mannered pastor, but I felt like those boots showed the world I wasn't too mild-mannered. However, they KILLED my feet. They were so painful I wanted to cry - but they looked SO good. I wore them on Sundays when I had three services every Sunday morning. I even wore them on Christmas Eve when we had FIVE services...until the Christmases of 2005 and 2006 when I was pregnant with my boys and my feet were swollen and didn't fit in my edgy boots. I wore comfortable shoes then.

I never wore the boots again. It's hard to go back once you allow yourself to be comfortable. When we moved away from Colorado, I left behind almost all my painful shoes. Letting them go wasn't hard by the time I did it.

We don't always let go because we choose it in the first place. Sometimes change is thrust upon us, and all we can do is look back upon it all afterward and sift through the memories to discern what were the blessings and what was the sadness in it.

While I used to see letting go as a difficult thing that I would not choose, as the years go by, I veer toward it more often. It feels good to make the journey lighter: letting go of possessions, letting go of a fussy hairstyle, letting go of a rigid make-up routine, letting go of always doing some process the same way. In fact, I have found that if I am paying attention, my life cries out to me to let go, be willing to be different, affected, less encumbered. These days, when I am feeling unusually tired or stressed, I pause and ask myself what it is that needs me to loosen my grip upon it. The answer doesn't come immediately, but if I gently keep asking myself, eventually the answer rises to the top of my thoughts.

Do you need to let go of something or someone? If the time is right for letting go, even if you are afraid, there will be a sense of lightness, freedom, and exhilaration to the thought of it. Listen to your heart and your smarts, be gentle and brave. Maybe you think you aren't strong enough to do it yourself, but that's okay. You don't have to be. As the angel Gabriel reminded Mary when he told her Jesus would be born, *"Nothing is impossible with God."*

"And did you know that your cousin Elizabeth conceived a son, old as she is? Everyone called her barren, and here she is six months pregnant! Nothing, you see, is impossible with God." (Luke 1:37)

Prayer: Dear God, help me loosen my grip on what no longer is beneficial and listen for Your guidance telling me what most deserves my time, attention, money, and energy. In Jesus name, I pray. Amen.

Reflect: Have you "let go" of anything recently? What were the joys and sorrows in that experience? What did you learn from it?

Eksjo Lutheran Church
Lake Park, Minnesota

Blue Christmas

The Blue Christmas service, usually held around the longest night of the year, is a time set aside for remembering and prayer. It is especially helpful for those who are having a hard time during the Christmas season. The holidays bring many emotions to the surface. Grief and depression can cut deep as the daylight gets shorter and shorter. At the Blue Christmas service, we gather to sing some contemplative songs, reflect, pray, and ask for God's healing balm on the hurting places. For us. For all.

In December of 2012, my church had our Christmas pageant at church as usual. There's nothing quite like hearing that old, old story of our Savior's birth being told by the youngest voices of the church.

We had rehearsals and got the costumes ready to go. The littlest children who had all been sheep and cows and chickens in the play in years past now wanted to have speaking parts, so we had five angels, seven shepherds, and a few extra wise men. There was a new baby born in our little congregation that year, so we were excited we even had someone to play the role of the baby Jesus.

It was a perfect evening with lovely weather. As we stood out on the steps before we went in, I thought about how it was one of those moments I wouldn't forget. I ran my gaze over the children in their costumes, laughing and talking in the twilight, and then glanced at the parents inside, poised with their cameras, ready to take pictures. You could practically see their hearts swelling with pride at their little shepherd, their little wise man, their little angel. The play went smoothly; we really couldn't have asked for a better evening.

But at the very same time, if you looked over near the altar, burning the silently was a long line of candles. We lighted them that morning in memory of other beautiful children, twenty of them, and their teachers who died that week when there was an attack on Sandy Hook Elementary School in Newtown, Connecticut.

Every week at the end of the children's sermon I say a prayer for the children that God would guide them and guard them. The Sunday after the shooting in Newtown, I repeated those words, but the words felt so heavy and strange. I thought about how Pastors and parents probably had always prayed for those dear children in Connecticut, too, and yet they spent that Christmas grieving unspeakable loss.

Faith in God is not a magic charm that keeps away bad things. Trust and belief in Christ is not some sort of guarantee that harm will not come. The steering wheel can still slip, the playground equipment can yet malfunction, the storm clouds could gather, the medicine can stop keeping the illness at bay at any time. We cannot manage the future or predict what will meet us as we step into each minute.

So, what do we do?

We cherish the now. We do not know what will come, but we give thanks for the blessings there are. I take a cue from Mary, the mother of Jesus here. One of my favorite verses from the Christmas story in the gospel of Luke is where all these things were happening the night that Jesus was born, and Mary was taking it all in. It reads, *"But Mary treasured all these things, pondering them in her heart." (Luke 2:19)* The wisest and happiest people are the ones who notice their blessings, take time to treasure the moments while they are happening.

Pause over your coffee, sit on the step when the breeze is just so, take the long way home, listen to your child's breathing – in and out, in and out – and whisper thanks to God. When we notice the loveliness of this world, that is the most excellent Hallelujah.

What else can we do?

We can trust that God is strong enough to hold the things we place in God's hands. When my mom was dying, my hometown pastor wrote to me, *"no matter what happens, Ruth, your mom is held in God's hands. And God's hands are strong."*

Those simple words meant so much to me. In mom's last months and days, there was nothing we could control. It felt like everything – her life, our time together, our hopes for healing – all of it was slipping right out of our grasp. I knew I was losing her. I knew the sadness of it all was going to be too much for me; I would disappear. I always used to say that nothing was real until I told Mom about it, so then after she died, nothing would be real anymore. The grief was crushing.

Those few words her pastor wrote to me provided me with an image of comfort during that time. In life and in death, she was held safe in God's hands forever. While there was nothing I could do to get through that dark time, and the sadness was going to be too much for me, I had a suspicion and a promise that it was not going to be too much for God. God's strong hands could hold me as well.

This is the message of hope that can carry us through the longest night and give us strength for seasons to come:

If it seems the illness has lasted too long and the healing will never happen, remember you are held in God's hands, and God's hands are strong.

When the worst thing has happened, and so much is broken you are sure you will never be whole again, remember you are held in God's hands, and God's hands are strong.

When the diagnosis is grim, when the way is scary, when the vows are shattered and lying in pieces on the ground, when it seems darkness is all that will ever be – remember you are held in God's hands, and God's hands are strong.

"But Mary treasured up all these things and pondered them in her heart."
– Luke 2:19

Prayer: Dear God, thank you for holding me and loving me through every season of this life. In Jesus name, I pray. Amen.

Reflect: What has been something comforting that someone has shared with you or done for you when you have been in a difficult time? Why was it helpful?

Saint Olaf's Kirke – "The Rock Church"
Cranfills Gap, Texas

Even If

There are two pivotal words in the Bible story of Shadrach, Meshach, and Abednego. The words are "even if."

If you grew up in the church, you likely have known this Bible story most of your life. Here's a quick recap:

Three Jewish young men, Shadrach, Meshach, and Abednego, refuse to bow down to a huge gold statue that the king has put in place to show off his power. The king demands all the officials come to the dedication of this statue and he commands that whenever people hear the sound of the horn, pipe, lyre, trigon (which was a triangular-shaped stringed instrument), harp and drum – they were to fall on their knees and worship the big golden statue.

So, all the instruments play and the people are falling to their knees to worship the statue when they hear them, but the king finds out that Shadrach, Meshach, and Abednego do not.

Shadrach, Meshach, and Abednego were not always known by these names. If you looked a little bit earlier in the book of Daniel, you would find that before this, their names were Hananiah, Mishael, and Azariah.

These young men were brought to work in the king's court and taught the language and literature of the Chaldeans. They were forced to give up their heritage and even their religious beliefs. Their original Jewish names had meanings: Hananiah meant "Who is like God," Mishael meant, "God is gracious", and Azariah meant, "God keeps him."

But now when they were brought into service in the king's court, their new names had references to Babylonian gods. For example, Abednego means "servant of Nego" – Nego was a Babylonian god. Now, not only are these young men expected to change their Jewish names, but now there is another attempt to compel these immigrants to change their religion and heritage as they are to bow down and worship the golden statue of the Emperor and to submit to his authority instead of the God of Israel.

They won't do it.

And the king is so angry. That's how leaders who are full of themselves get when people aren't doing what they want – they throw tantrums. The king says, "if you don't worship you'll immediately be thrown into a furnace of blazing fire; and who is the god who will deliver you out of my hands?"

Shadrach, Meshach, and Abednego say, "We don't need to defend ourselves to you, O king. Our God is able to deliver us out of the fire – but *even if* he doesn't, we will never serve your golden statue you have set up."

Even if.

I was listening to a story told by the lead singer of the Christian band, Mercy Me, Bart Millard. He was talking about how one of his children was diagnosed with Type 1 diabetes at age two. His family has learned how to handle this challenge, and that child is now 13 so Bart estimates that his son has had over 37,000 insulin shots in his life – because any time he eats, he needs an injection. It will likely always be this way.

He was telling about a day when the reality of his son's chronic illness was getting him down more than usual, and he felt weighed down by his worries for his son. He and his son and wife had just left the doctor's office, and they ran into a woman from church. She asked what they were up to and he told her they had just been to the doctor to get the 6-month check-up on their boy's diabetes and the woman said, "I'm going to pray for healing for him, and I'll have my church pray for him, too."

He explained how at that moment, his gut reaction wasn't gratitude, but anger. He thought to himself, *"Like that never occurred to me – to pray for healing for my son. I pray every day for that. I know God can heal him, but God hasn't. And that is okay."* He talked about how his family and his son have learned how to thrive in spite of the illness, and they believe that somehow, in some way God will work through that illness to bless the lives of others through their son. But then he shook his head and admitted it doesn't feel okay every day.

He talked about how he wants to always be like Shadrach, Meshach, and Abednego and say, "I know God is able to heal – but even if God doesn't, I will serve no other god." Sometimes he does that with his whole heart as he sings praise music in front of churches and stadiums, but sometimes he isn't able to do that. It is then that he leans hard on Jesus and trusts in Jesus' strength to get him through.

It was a beautiful witness as he talked about a song he wrote called "Even If".

I pray that God gives us that "even if" kind of faith that helps us remember that God isn't a genie to grant our wishes. Rather, God is with us in the fire, and we can trust that. Even if and when the worst happens. Even if healing doesn't come. Even if we mess up bad. Even if, and no matter what – our hope is in Christ alone.

When my Mom was dying, I knew I was losing her, and my heart was breaking. When the nurses needed to take her for a test or get her cleaned up, I would go for walks on the path around the outside of the hospital. I walked and cried and walked some more. I didn't have any words to pray, but out of nowhere in the middle of the despair, old hymn lyrics would come to mind.

"When peace like a river attendeth my way
When sorrows like sea billows roll
Whatever my lot thou hast taught me to say
It is well, it is well with my soul."
(from the Hymn, "When Peace Like a River" by Horatio Gates Spafford, 1873)

It was mysterious and comforting and haunting. God kept singing to me in the fire of that loss, never letting the reassuring songs leave my mind even as I suffered, even as I knew I had to let go.

Even if. Even if and when the worst happens, God is with you in the fire.

Shadrach, Meshach, and Abednego answered King Nebuchadnezzar, "Your threat means nothing to us. If you throw us in the fire, the God we serve can rescue us from your roaring furnace and anything else you might cook up, O king. But even if he doesn't, it wouldn't make a bit of difference, O king. We still wouldn't serve your gods or worship the gold statue you set up."- Daniel 3:16-18 The Message (MSG)

Prayer: Dear God, help me to trust in you alone no matter what comes. In Jesus' name, I pray. Amen.

Reflect: Has there been a difficult time in your life in which you felt God's presence especially close?

The abandoned Bethania Lutheran Church
Purley, Minnesota

Christ Still Comes: A Message for Christmas Day

Advent has come and gone; the candlelight of Christmas Eve is over, and here we are in the bright light of Christmas day.

To tell you the truth it all snuck up on me. We recently moved into a different house and we still haven't uncovered the Christmas ornaments or lights. You wouldn't know it is Christmas at our home unless you saw the spectacular decorations on our next-door neighbor's house.

It is surprising to me that even though we've made our way through Advent and lit the candles on the Advent wreath one by one, I wasn't quite ready for Christmas to arrive. Frankly, even now I'm not all that filled with what anyone would recognize as Christmas spirit. I've had a cold all week and yesterday as I scuffled my way from the parking lot into the church I was in a sour mood. I couldn't find the right outfit to wear, my hair had turned out wrong, the cat had thrown up on the kitchen floor, and my head was full of congestion. And worse than that, I felt guilty that I was in such a bad mood on the morning of Christmas Eve. No matter how hard I tried, I couldn't shift my gaze from myself to that manger. No matter how much I wanted to be full of Christmas cheer, my demeanor better suited Good Friday.

I wonder if you have ever felt that way during the Christmas season? Have you ever felt like if you could just pause for a moment and catch your breath you might be able to enjoy this time of year a little more, but there is too much to do: too many people to see, gatherings to attend, gifts to buy and cookies to bake? Have you ever felt like it's too hard to dig through the wrapping paper, tinsel and colored lights to even begin to find the real meaning of the holiday? Wouldn't it be nice if we could put off Christmas until we were ready for it? Until a time when everything was in place, and we all felt like celebrating?

Well, that is how I felt. But Christmas came anyway. It came in spite of me.

A friend of mine told me a story about her young daughter who is fascinated with the little green plastic army figures that belong to her brothers. Her daughter picks up these army figures and moves them around the house, and so my friend said she wasn't surprised when a few weeks ago she noticed in her family nativity scene, there wasn't just Mary and Joseph, but four little army men pointing their guns in every direction. She went to take them out, but then she thought perhaps it wasn't an unfair representation of Jesus' coming into the world. Jesus was not born into a world free of violence or hate. He was not born into a perfect world – he was born into our world as it was, and he still comes into our lives, right now, just as we are.

We dress up our houses and ourselves and pour all sorts of time and effort into creating just the right holiday and just the right kind of Christmas cheer, but Jesus came for Scrooge just as much as Tiny Tim. He came just as much for the antagonist as the protagonist, as much for the villain as the hero, as much for the person you like the least, as for the person you love the most.

We gather to celebrate Christmas and the good news of Jesus' birth, but the best news is that he came even for those who cannot or will not celebrate his birth. That is wondrous love. A love that though we may search for it, finds us all along.

One Christmas break from college when I was around 20 years old, instead of going home or to a friend's house or staying at school and working, I went out to visit my old Bible camp by myself.

I didn't tell anyone where I was going. It was supposed to be my secret pilgrimage. I sat and wrote in my journal by firelight. I read and prayed and looked forward to seeing what kind of enlightenment some days of solitude and silence would bring.

On Christmas day, I was sitting by the window overlooking the lake when the phone on the wall just above my head rang. After days of complete quiet except for the sound of the wind blowing across the frozen lake, the jolt of the telephone nearly scared me out of my skin. After bolting straight out of my chair and across the room, I stepped calmly back toward the phone and picked up the receiver.

It was my mom calling. I don't know how she tracked me down but, she called just to say, "Merry Christmas" and "I love you." In retrospect, I shouldn't have been surprised she could find me. She knew that camp was my favorite place in the world and it made sense that's where I would go if I wanted to be alone.

After I hung up the phone, the quiet of that place was deafening. I packed up my stuff to go to my parents' house. I realized there was nothing I was going to find by putting myself apart from everyone. Although I had listened for God in the sound of the trees and the silence of the snow dancing across the ice-covered lake, it wasn't my searching that brought me closer to any great understanding. Instead, the things I needed to find were looking for me all along. What I needed had been knit into my life from the very start.

What does all this mean? It means that Christmas day is a time to remember we don't need to worry so much about the searching because we have already been found. Christ comes to us again and again. "Emmanuel" means God with us. God with us in so many ways! Christ comes to us in parents, in each other, in strangers, in words that startle and amaze us, in the sacraments we share, and in a manger. Christ comes to us though we may not feel ready or happy or sane. Christ comes to us just as we are.

"Look, the virgin shall conceive and bear a son, and they shall name him Emmanuel," which means, "God is with us." – Matthew 1:23 NRSV

Prayer: Thank you, God, for coming to be born among us and within us through Jesus. Thank you for the joy and mystery of Christmas. In Jesus' name, I pray. Amen.

Reflect: Has there been a time when you realized you weren't nearly as lost as you thought you were?

Waves of snow at Saint Peter's Lutheran Church
Audubon, Minnesota

Christmas Light

By the time we get to December 25th, most people are ready to start taking down all the Nativity sets and Christmas lights. Even in the church, we are itching to stop singing the carols and get the poinsettias out of the building. We've read the Christmas story, we've sung Silent Night, now we are left looking around and wondering, are we done? Or is there still something left here to astonish us?

Back in college, my two closest friends were from Montana. During spring break our freshman year, one of those friends, Kaia, invited me to go home with her to Billings. I thought that sounded fun and I had never seen the mountains, so off we went.

We caught a ride with a senior named Darren. We chipped in some money for gas and piled into his tiny yellow Toyota pick-up for the 12-hour drive from Moorhead to Billings. His little truck would slow down to about 40 mph on every hill. He loved John Denver, Jim Croce, and the Carpenters so we listened to them the whole way. Still, whenever I hear "Rocky Mountain High" or "We've Only Just Begun," I think about that long drive.

We arrived in Billings on a cloudy evening. The next day, Kaia's father had arranged for a little trip for the whole family and me to go up into the mountains to ski. The weather was still cloudy as we drove and it was dark as we pulled into the lodge where we were going to stay for the night. As we unloaded the car, Kaia's dad said to me, "Well, Ruth, you are in the mountains now!" – but with the overcast sky, the darkness and the snow, it looked the same as anywhere else.

The next morning when I woke up I could see the sun was shining – and blue sky peeking through the curtains. I scurried to the window to look outside and there they were – peaks erupting from the ground in every direction. Even though they had been there when I fell asleep, the darkness had kept me from seeing them. But now, in the light, my surroundings were no longer a mystery. It's amazing how the light changes things.

The gospel of John talks about how the light changes everything: the light of the Word coming into the world – Jesus. *"He was in the beginning with God. In him was life, and the life was the light of all people. That light shines in the darkness, and the darkness has not overcome it."* (John 1:4-5)

What difference does that light of Christ, make to us? Will following that light, like a star, guide us to places beyond our dreaming?

You see, there is something left to astonish us as Christmas Day dawns. You've heard the message that we have a Savior who chose to come to us just as we are: to the saints and sinners, the crabby and the joyful, the honest and the cheaters, the nice and the cruel. Now hear this: while he came to us just as we are, his presence isn't going to leave us that way. He's more than a light, he is fire, refining us, perfecting us in fits and starts and in spite of ourselves.

This Christmas stuff may seem tame and comforting, the same carols, the same sweet story about a baby king and a manger year after year. But if you are feeling brave, stick around and see the revolution he has come to lead in your life.

Maybe we're ready for the peanut brittle, the reindeer, the twinkling lights, the Christmas tree and the ornaments to be gone. That's okay because those things have their time and place. They come and go with the season. But if we arrive at Christmas Day seeking the light of Christ to shine in and through our lives, then it's just as the Carpenters sang, "we've only just begun."

> *1-2 The Word was first,*
> *the Word present to God,*
> *God present to the Word.*
> *The Word was God,*
> *in readiness for God from day one.*
>
> *3-5 Everything was created through him;*
> *nothing—not one thing!—*

came into being without him.
What came into existence was Life,
and the Life was Light to live by.
The Life-Light blazed out of the darkness;
the darkness couldn't put it out. – John 1:1-5 (The Message MSG)

Prayer: Dear God, be our light in the darkness. Always. In Jesus name, we pray. Amen.

Reflect: Do you want Jesus to lead a revolution in your life? What sounds good about that? What sounds scary about that?

South Immanuel Lutheran Church
Rothsay, Minnesota

Happy New Year

When my younger son, Jesse, was only about three months old, my mom became very sick and was sent to the hospital in Saint Cloud, Minnesota. I couldn't stand the thought of her being in the hospital a couple hours from family and friends with no one able to visit her regularly, so I squeezed in some vacation time to come up to Minnesota to be with her. I brought Jesse with me, our other son stayed at home with Chad in Colorado, and each day Jesse and I would spend as much time with mom in the hospital as we could.

As I sat by mom's bedside holding Jesse, I thought about the stark contrasts of my life just then. There I was holding this brand new little person, who was round-cheeked, full of health and smiles and new beginnings. Next to me was mom, grayish and weary with tubes coming out of her arms, full of sickness and seeming very much to be at the end of her days. It struck me how beautiful and broken life could be all at the same time. Joy and sorrow co-existing.

On Christmas, in the Christian church we gather around the manger with carols and candlelight. The scripture readings sing of Light and Love coming into the world – pure joy and beauty.

And just a week later, in many churches the Gospel reading is from the second chapter of Matthew: King Herod, full of fear and jealousy, wanting to protect his throne from this infant king has put out a hit on all the children two years old and under in and around Bethlehem. Pure brokenness and horror.

It turns out the Christmas season can hold its' share of joy and sorrow as well.

King Herod ruled in Judea for 37 years. He built fortresses, aqueducts, theatres, and other public buildings and generally raised the prosperity of his land. There was a dark and cruel streak in Herod's character that showed itself increasingly as he grew older. He was prone to intense jealousy, and it is recorded that his mind was so poisoned against one of his wives, Mariamne, that he murdered her, her two sons, her brother, her grandfather, and her mother.

He sent the wise men, gifted astrologers, to search for the baby Jesus and when they found him they were to send word back to King Herod. He told them he wanted to pay homage to this baby king as well. After the wise men found Jesus and brought him the famed gifts of gold, frankincense, and myrrh, they were warned in a dream not to return to Herod. Herod's darkness overcame him when he found out that the wise men didn't do as he told them. Rage fills him, and that is when he calls for the murder of the children.

This story, sometimes known as "The Slaughter of the Innocents," only told by Saint Matthew in the Bible, is never mentioned anywhere else in any historical records. Some historians question if it really happened. Others say that it likely happened but the number of children of that age in and around Bethlehem was such a small number, perhaps less than twenty, that it was not recorded by other historians.

It strikes me as profoundly fitting and haunting that Matthew telling this story even as we still bask in the glow of the Christmas season. No matter how much we have tried to sanitize and tame the story of the birth of Jesus, turn it into a sweet story about a baby in a manger, the truth is that he was born into a world of sin. A place that then, as now, holds its' share of both startling beauty and unspeakable darkness. He was born to be Light in that darkness. To be hope when all other hope seems lost.

Is he light in your darkness? Does God's word bring you comfort and peace in times of distress? Do you find strength for your days and wisdom for your journey as you kneel at the foot of the cross? Do you long for more light, more comfort, peace, and strength?

If you are hoping to feed your Spirit in this new year, to feel more plugged in to the Source of Life – there are some valuable practices that will help you with that goal:

Pray: make a daily practice of talking to and listening for God. Devote time to meditation and stillness.

You know how when someone is trying to speak to you, but if you aren't paying attention or only half-listening, you miss it? That's how it is when we don't make time for prayer and devotion in our days. God is always speaking to us, but much of the time we aren't paying attention, we are so busy running from one thing to the next, filling our minds with noise, making lists, and checking our phones, that we leave hardly any room for the Spirit to move.

Recently, I went to the eye doctor and I brought a book with me for while I was waiting. Over the course of the appointment I was ushered from one room to the next, and at one point, they dilated my eyes and I had to sit for a bit while unable to focus on anything. I couldn't read my book. I couldn't check my phone. I could only sit there quietly. It is moments like that when I realize how seldom I am still and quiet without doing, reading or watching something. I'm always filling in those spaces.

Did you know it was in dreams that God gave a message to Joseph to tell him to take his family and flee, to become refugees, immigrants in a strange land, because they were in danger? It was also in a dream when Joseph was informed that Jesus would be born. Dreams and visions (which are dreams while awake) were written about often in the Bible. God used visions and dreams to communicate with people. In fact, when there was a lack of dreams or visions among the people, it meant that something was wrong, that people weren't paying attention to God.

There are at least 39 times in the Bible when God spoke to people through dreams and visions. God didn't just speak to people of old, God is still speaking to us and through us. The only question is, are we listening?

Monks set aside hours for lectio divina, "spiritual reading". However, even we non-monks need to make time for transcendent matters such as beauty, creativity, service, faith, but too often these get pushed aside for more urgent demands, and life begins to feel empty and purposeless. If you don't already, find a way to daily make time to listen, be still, and pray.

Serve: the second excellent way to feed your spirit is to find a way to serve. Partly because there are countless places and people that need help, but mostly because you need it. God put us here not just to get through our days and collect as many material things as possible while we do it, but to make those days matter.

Martin Luther King, Jr. wrote, *"Everybody can be great...because anybody can serve. You don't have to have a college degree to serve. You don't have to make your subject and verb agree to serve. You only need a heart full of grace. A soul generated by love."*

And while you are at it, be sure to get to know those you are serving. Learn about them, laugh and share yourself with them, because this is what breaks down the countless walls that divide us.

As Jesus came to be Light in our darkness, every day we can be light in the darkness for others. What magnificent, beautiful, and holy work in which we get to participate.

Another new year begins — fill it with prayer and service. Do that, and there's a better than average chance it will indeed be a happy new year.

13 Now after they had left, an angel of the Lord appeared to Joseph in a dream and said, "Get up, take the child and his mother, and flee to Egypt, and remain there until I tell you; for Herod is about to search for the child, to destroy him." – Matthew 2:13

Prayer: Today, spend a few minutes in complete silence. Listen to your breathing. If a thought comes to mind, notice it, and then go back to paying attention to your breathing. This practice of mindfulness, especially when done for a few minutes each day can be very calming and help with concentration and focus.

Reflect: What is one way you can include more prayer time in your life this week? What is one way you can include more service to others in your life this week?

Saint Peter's Lutheran Church and Sun Dogs
Audubon, Minnesota

Smooth, Shiny Stones

January in Minnesota is like the end of July in Texas. The weather is unforgiving, but there is still plenty of beauty if you choose to see it. In Texas, that beauty used to sneak up on me when a rare cool breeze would sweep in by surprise during an evening walk in the cemetery or when the boys and I would go outside after dark and lie down on the cement basketball court and stare up at the stars. The cement would still be hot from soaking up the sun all day long. We would lie there in the warm night air and watch for shooting stars, talk, and laugh until one of us wondered out loud if the rattlesnakes liked to come out at night, too. Then, we would get up and make our way back inside into the cool, air-conditioned comfort of the parsonage.

Now, in these Minnesota winters, there is loveliness in the sun sparkling off the snow, even though by the end of January we've mostly stopped commenting on it. Too many of us are daydreaming about warmer weather to spend much time remarking on the beauty of a new snowfall or even the shocking splendor of the sundogs that come out to hover near the sun. No, these days we are more likely to see beauty in moments like I had yesterday when a friend stopped by when I was outside the church and we stood in the parking lot for nearly fifteen minutes to talk – no hats, no gloves – and the air didn't even hurt our faces! It was only eleven degrees, but it felt like Springtime was crawling up the hill toward us. January in Minnesota, like the end of July in Texas, you get grateful for the small favors that weather tosses your way.

Today I went to visit an elderly lady in my congregation. She lives in a farmhouse not very far from our church, the same church where she has worshipped her whole life. Her dogs came scrambling over to greet me as I got out of my car, sniffing my hands and my legs before losing interest and heading over to check out my car.

I visit people in their homes often, usually because they are no longer able to get out and about for one reason or another. I used to sometimes struggle with doing these visits early in my ministry. The list of homebound members was long and I found it daunting to visit that many people regularly and make a connection with them. I felt overwhelmed at the task of all those conversations and bringing communion to people who were dealing with much that was outside my understanding. At the beginning of my years as a pastor I wasn't married with kids. I was young, single, and interested in my gym membership, making friends, writing, and finishing my doctorate. While I cared about the homebound folks I visited, there was so much I couldn't comprehend about their medications, doctor visits, concerns for their grown children and dwindling days.

It wasn't until shortly before my father died that I began to see the visits I do every day in a different light. It was then that I noticed that my parents, from whom I had been living far away for many years as I served different churches, were getting to be the same age as my homebound members. I started to look across the living rooms at the people I was visiting and notice a walker that was just like the kind I got for my dad on my last visit home, or someone's skin had the same pale, translucent appearance that mom was getting.

That was when I began to really see the people I was visiting. I'm sad to say it took me so long, but I couldn't come to maturity in that until I finally did. As a daughter who grieved the changes and losses my parents were going through, I became better at listening to the changes and losses of my aging parishioners.

I grieved I wasn't near my parents to be more helpful to them during their final years. I thought about how every day I visited the elderly, but I couldn't frequently visit those who needed me the most, my own family.

I didn't plan it that way. As much as I always wanted to live other places and was glad that God brought me where God did, I pictured a time would come again when I would be able to be near my parents and journey with them through their final days. But time went by, and I was busy – busy with work, busy with my babies, and while I spoke to my mom on the phone nearly every day, what she didn't mention was that time was running out. I did try more than a few times to get back to be a pastor at a church in Minnesota, but no doors opened.

So, for fifteen years I served in New York, Colorado, and Texas, all the while getting farther and farther from home. Dad died when we were in Colorado. Mom died while we were in Texas. I no longer had to wonder what they were doing as I went about my daily visits to other peoples' parents. But now as I tended the gravestones in my church cemetery, I wished I could plant flowers and pull weeds from the gravestones of my parents. I couldn't help but think about how I failed them in their final years and now in death, too.

I see everything in ministry differently now than I did when I started. I am well-acquainted with the beauty of this clergy life, but also the sorrow.

When I think of all the cups of coffee shared, the foreheads of babies I have blessed and baptized, the dying I have commended into God's care, the ways that prayer and mission are part of the fabric of my days, I'm overwhelmed with gratitude. Nevertheless, the loss of time with my aging parents due to following this path is the one shiny, smooth stone of sadness and regret I carry with me when I think about the years that have passed. Perhaps it made me a better pastor, because now I understand as I couldn't before that every single one of us has shiny, smooth stones which weigh us down. I may not know what yours are, but I know you have some. Life gives each of us our share.

And so sometimes people let me visit them in their homes, or their hospital rooms or nursing home to pray over those smooth, shiny stones. On this January day in rural Minnesota, with the sun sparkling off the snow as I drove along prairie roads, I did that.

> *When you pass through the waters, I will be with you;*
> *and through the rivers, they shall not overwhelm you;*
> *when you walk through fire you shall not be burned,*
> *and the flame shall not consume you. – Isaiah 43:2 NRSV*

Prayer: Dear God, it is often said that timing is everything. Maybe that is why it hurts so much when we run out of time to do and say the things we always planned on doing and saying. When I don't understand why things turn out the way they do, grant me your peace that passes all understanding. In Jesus' name, I pray. Amen.

Reflect: What do you understand very differently now than you did twenty years ago? Do you think it could have been possible for you to achieve that understanding earlier or are there some things you simply must "live into"?

Windswept Road
Northwestern Minnesota

Evangelism

What comes to mind for you when you hear the word "evangelism"? Do you think about street corner preachers calling out phrases such as "repent and be saved"? Do you get a picture in your mind of the television evangelist in an expensive suit on the stage of a stadium-sized church?

Do you think of yourself? In truth, all Christians are called to be evangelists, and yet many would steer far from calling ourselves such a thing. Perhaps that is because many times we have witnessed evangelism done so poorly.

I think of a clear and cold winter day back in the mid-nineties. My car broke down on a freeway in North Dakota, and a man and his wife stopped to pick me up and bring me to the nearest phone. I was thankful for their kindness, and we chatted as we shared in that short time together. They asked me where I was from and what I did. At the time, I was a student in seminary studying to be a pastor, and I told them so. Their response was one that by then I had gotten used to as they began to evangelize to me about how I was misled; that it was sinful for any woman to presume she could be a pastor, and that they would be praying for me that God would point me back on the right path. I sighed and politely thanked them for the ride. I knew by then that they were just two of many, many people who interpreted scripture in such a way. There was nothing I was going to be able to say in such a short amount of time that would change their mind.

But I wondered why they thought they could change my mind. Did they imagine that what they were saying was going to be entirely new information? Did they think that by the end of the car ride I would abandon religious studies after years and years of pursuit? Did they think I could just toss the calling placed on my heart since the age of fourteen, a calling affirmed and nurtured by my pastors, my churches, and my family who taught me not only a love of scripture but to understand and live in the life-giving faith and grace found in Jesus Christ? Did they imagine their few words were going to strip away all of that?

What that couple tried to do that day, while I'm sure it was well-meaning, was hollow and alienating. It took into account nothing about me or my journey of faith or my understanding of who God was and is. They were trying squish me into their idea of what a Christian really should be like in the time it took to travel over a few windswept Dakota miles. I resented it.

And that sort of thing, unfortunately, is the first thing that comes to my mind when I think of the word 'evangelism'.

We can take some positive evangelism lessons from John the Baptist. When he sees Jesus, he can't help but tell others about his experience, *"Here he is, God's Passover Lamb! He forgives the sins of the world! This is the man I've been talking about, 'the One who comes after me but is really ahead of me.' "I watched the Spirit, like a dove flying down out of the sky, making himself at home in him. That's exactly what I saw happen, and I'm telling you, there's no question about it: This is the Son of God."* (John 1:35, 32) John is so excited and overwhelmed by what he has seen, his joy spills out. When others hear what he says, they feel compelled to follow Jesus, too. They want to experience some of the wonder that John is feeling in knowing Jesus.

John the Baptist was a great evangelist because a synonym of the word evangelize is "Proclaim". He joyfully and loudly proclaimed who Jesus was and by doing so, he drew others to Jesus. Some can do that. Have you known people like that whose love for the Lord is infectious; their thirst and hunger to know God is so beautiful, humbling, and passionate that it makes others want to have a closer walk with God? That can be a beautiful form of evangelism, to be so in love with God and so devoted to learning as much as we can and serving as much as we can that we are consumed by love and we can't help but share that joy we have found.

However, the difficulty of trying to be this kind of evangelist is that very few of us are always spilling over with our passion for faith. Life gets full and complicated. There are dishes to do and the cat needs to be taken to the vet, there are appointments to keep, and the constant buzz and hum of life can easily overpower our inclination toward always having our thoughts turned toward God.

So, we can take comfort in knowing there is an even more powerful way of being an evangelist - an approach that draws us gently together and creates a space for the Spirit of God to enter.

And it is all about relationships - but not in the way we might initially think about relationships and evangelism. Often when we talk about relationships and evangelism in the church, we think of them as a means to an end. For example, we worry about attendance and so we say, "invite your friends to church" and we think that will help fill in some of the empty spaces. We worry about church finances and so we say, "we need more people to come so then we will have more people giving." Or perhaps that couple I met back on the road in North Dakota was worried because the ways God had called me to serve challenged what they were taught about what was right, and so they needed to point out my error of thinking and set me on the right path.

Too often in the church when we think about evangelism and relationships we think of doing so as a means toward something else in the end. As it says in the book, "Relational Pastor" by Andrew Root, *"We have deeply wanted our ministry to be relational, but not for the sake of persons, for the sake of ministry, for the sake of initiatives. In other words, we have wanted people to be relationally connected so that they might come to what we are offering or believe what we are preaching or teaching."* This is human nature and we all fall into this way of thinking sometimes, this selfish evangelism, one that focuses on a goal somewhere off in the distance, not on that person and that relationship right here and right now.

How would it be to think of the relationship as our only goal - not so that we can have them come to church someday or get them to think about Jesus like we do, but just so that we can know them and they can know us? What if that was our only goal? Could that possibly be evangelism at its finest?

I think of the first Bible camp counselor I ever had. Her name was Beth. I was a shy kid, uncomfortable in my skin, deeply uncool. She liked to tell us stories, sometimes about Jesus but sometimes just about life. Every night at bedtime, she hugged each of us goodnight and as she did so, she whispered to us that Jesus loved us. It was powerful and welcome. I would lie there in the dark and think about it. *Jesus loves me. Beth said so. And mom and dad say so. Grandma says so. And if these people who take time for me and care about me want me to know about Jesus' love, then it must be something.*

Over time, the background noise of people telling me about Jesus' love for me became a song, the dearest thing I had ever heard. It was not a sudden thing, it was not because of a moment or a single person, and it was never because of anyone trying to win me over for any cause or goal other than they wanted to know me and for me to know them. And to know them was to know they loved Jesus. Because of them and their care and the witness of their very lives, I fell in love with him, too.

Being evangelical will only start to sound like a welcome thing when we realize what it is. It is sharing faith, yet only sometimes with words. Sometimes it is sharing faith through a powerful and positive verbal witness of Jesus Christ. Sometimes it is sharing Jesus' love through simple actions - like taking some food over to your neighbor after a surgery. It might be pausing, even though you had so much to do, long enough to sit down and listen when you encountered someone who was heartbroken.

It's sacred when wants time with you, whether going for a walk down the road or hearing someone say, "come on over sometime" or sharing a cup of coffee. There's a reason these things feel like they matter because they do. It's time shared; it's life shared, it's why when those disciples caught up to Jesus and they asked him where he was going, he didn't just tell them where he was headed, he said, "Come along and see for yourself." Jesus was modeling evangelism for us right there.

In the church, we might do well to focus less on what the fruit of building relationships might be and more on just being present with one another: at work, at home, at the grocery store, and wherever we go. Be a gentle presence, interested in others, listen without judgment, hear the stories others bear, and share yours. Trust that in ways we don't know and may never see, God will work through us to bring others to Christ.

So, go on and be evangelical. Proclaim Jesus through your words and through your lives. Love and live in Jesus' name.

> 35 The next day John was there again with two of his disciples. 36 When he saw Jesus passing by, he said, "Look, the Lamb of God!"
> 37 When the two disciples heard him say this, they followed Jesus. 38 Turning around, Jesus saw them following and asked, "What do you want?"
> They said, "Rabbi" (which means "Teacher"), "where are you staying?"
> 39 "Come," he replied, "and you will see." – John 1:35-39

Prayer: Dear God, help me proclaim your goodness and grace through what I say and do. Help me to really get to know the people you put in my life and see them with your loving eyes. In Jesus name, I pray. Amen.

Reflect: Who has been most influential to you on your journey of faith? Why?

An Everyday Prayer
Dear God,
I yelled at the dog
I had a cookie for breakfast
I was impatient with the children
I sighed over another cold, snowy day
I worried, and worried, and worried some more.
Countless times I lose my way as your follower each day.
Countless ways I wander in the darkness
So much for being a light in the world for you.
So much for showing others the way to you when so often I am distracted,
Disturbed,
Day-dreaming,
Dead-tired.
But still, you are here. For me, for all of us.
But still, I hear your breath in the evening breeze.
But still, your wonder is painted in the sunrise.
But still, you are everywhere – in the warm handshake on the way into church,
In the sweet smiles of children listening to stories about you.
In their squirminess, too.
You are here – in this holy place – so old, and yet being made new each year.
You are here – loving us at our best, holding us at our worst.
So thank you, God. Thank you for this day – snow and cold and all.
Thank you for blessing us with relationships, people to love. Help us to be better at that.
Thank you for all there is to do and be each day
but help us to not take it all so seriously that we miss the joy of the journey.
Thank you, thank you, thank you, God.
In Jesus' name, I pray.
Amen.

Grove Lake Lutheran Church
Pelican Rapids, Minnesota

Hometown

I went home yesterday. Well, the place that used to be my home. It's about 55 miles from where I live now – a tiny town of about 700 people – Henning, Minnesota.

It's like many small towns in this area – a school, a post office, some businesses and more churches than it probably needs. Most of the places there that hold my memories are virtually unrecognizable to me now. My grandmother's house was sold a few years ago, and the new owner has painted it a garish blue. The school built an addition shortly after I left and even my lovely little white church has been torn down, and a new, modern worship structure has taken its place.

I drove across the roads that wound themselves between lakes and woods, snow skittering across the highways in the temperatures that hovered near zero toward the place that once was home. I saw the school bus dropping off kids near Ottertail, drove past the areas where many of my classmates used to live – the classmates who lived on the "other side" of town from me. The lake kids.

I went to see mom and dad. I hadn't been there for many months. Although cemeteries are rarely full of fun, they are particularly desolate during the winter. When the weather is pleasant, I enjoy walking among the gravestones, observing the flowers blooming, the decorations and solar garden lights people have left behind for loved ones. During the winter, however, the cemetery is bitter and cold. I could only stand by their graves for a few minutes. I brushed some snow off their names engraved in the granite, a few tears freezing at the corners of my eyes, and then I shuffled back to the shelter of my car.

I drove around a bit more, but it only takes all of five minutes to drive down every street of Henning. Then, I pulled up to the assisted living home where my mom's best friend lives. It was about four o'clock in the afternoon, likely a good time to catch her. Norma was sitting in her room when I arrived. She makes a fuss over me when I come. I like that. Mom used to make a fuss over me, and I miss that. We sat and talked about this and that, and shared some memories about my mom and dad. It's a beautiful, bittersweet thing to talk to other people who miss the same people as you.

Finally, it was getting to be supper time, and the sun was going down. I hugged Norma goodbye and said I would be back soon when the weather gets warmer. She went into her big closet and brought out some chocolates for me to bring to the boys. She makes a fuss over them, too. I like that.

I left town as the sun set. I saw the water tower, the prairie, the sidewalks where my best friend, Michelle, and I used to walk and laugh until our sides hurt, the café where mom and I liked to have pie and coffee.

I hardly cry about her anymore. She's slipping from my daily memories and yet she's always there. I hear her in my voice, I see her in my mirror, she rests in the background of every decision I make. *What would mom think? What would she say? I miss you, I miss you, I miss you.*

Past the snowy fields I made my way back toward the place life has brought me now. The moon was rising bright and cold. I drove up to my warm house – the lights welcoming me home. My husband and children were in the midst of the evening routine. I could hear Owen practicing his baritone as I got out of the car. Jesse was wrestling with his math homework. Chad was putting away the leftovers from supper.

This beautiful life. These days so near and yet so exceedingly far from my hometown.

> *5 You have made my days a mere handbreadth;*
> *the span of my years is as nothing before you.*
> *Everyone is but a breath,*
> *even those who seem secure.*

Psalm 29:5 New International Version (NIV)

Prayer: Dear God, time is flying. Help me live fully in this day and treasure everything while there is still time. In Jesus name, I pray. Amen.

Reflect: Do you feel you have allowed yourself to fully grieve the losses you have experienced in life? Is there anything about your past losses that keep you from moving forward?

Good Shepherd Lutheran Church Cemetery
Henning, Minnesota

<u>Jesus, age 12</u>

Every year Jesus' parents went to Jerusalem for the festival of the Passover. The festival lasted seven days and included special meals and sacrifices as people remembered how God helped the Children of Israel escape slavery in Egypt.

When the gospel of Luke tells of this event, Jesus is twelve years old. It comes time to leave the festival, and Jesus' parents assume he is somewhere in the group of travelers and they end up leaving without him. By the time they realize he is gone and come back for him, they have been separated from him for days.

I hear this story with different ears as a mother than I did before I had children of my own. Since having children, whenever I read this story all I can think is "Ummm...Mary and Joseph, you traveled a day's journey before you even realized you were missing a child?"

But then I remember that there were relatives and many close friends traveling in the group, and it is possible that even the definition of family was much more elastic then, possibly everyone in the group was looking out for one another's kids. That's not so strange. I see that sort of thing even today in the churches I have served. If parents are busy in the kitchen or doing something else, others watch over the kiddos on the playground or Christian Education areas. But still, I wonder how Mary and Joseph must have felt when they realized that they traveled a day's journey before they noticed their son was missing?

Most parents experience at one time or another that sinking feeling of not knowing exactly where their child is - whether it is for just a few moments or much longer. The feeling is terrifying.

When my boys were very small, I took them to the mall to pick up something at the last minute before Christmas. Usually when we went shopping I put them in their double stroller to keep them contained, but that day I didn't want to drag the stroller out of the car so I let them walk and said, "Now, stay close to me."

This was before I fully understood that children have their own agendas and are surprisingly quick on their little legs. I looked away from them for a nanosecond as one boy ran one way, and the other ran the other way among the tall racks of clothing. I looked down where they had been, and they were just gone. I looked all around the racks right around me; I couldn't spot them anywhere! I began to search more frantically and it was probably only about twenty seconds until I heard them snickering – they were hiding among the clothes on one rack right next to me – but it felt like an eternity. For any parent, losing track of your child and not knowing where they are or what might be happening to them is awful.

Mary and Joseph returned to Jerusalem to look for Jesus. They didn't find him right away; it took them three days. He was sitting with the teachers, listening to them and asking them questions.

The reunion with his parents was not touching or sentimental. Mary says what she has probably been rehearsing for three days, *"Child, why have you treated us like this? Look, your father and I have been searching for you with great anxiety!" (Luke 2:48)* Jesus doesn't apologize. He is not the repentant son. Rather, he says, *"Why were you searching for me? Did you not know that I must be in my Father's house?"*

We don't know if his tone was matter-of-fact or petulant, but I always wonder if Mary felt a little like her head was going to explode at this point? We also don't know if she said anything else, such as, "I don't want to hear it, you are grounded for a month!" Or did she just hug her boy close, grateful she could hold him and see him again, even though she didn't understand him and what he was saying.

Take notice that here, once again, the scripture reminds us Mary treasured all these things in her heart (Luke 2:51). Just as she did the night he was born, and the angel choirs sang, and the shepherds came running to meet him – now, once again, twelve years later she is treasuring these things in her heart.

Of course, that is what parents do. Whether our children are the first-born of God or not, we treasure them, or as another version of this scripture reads, we hold them 'dearly and deeply'. From their amazing first breath to their astounding first steps to their incredible first words and as they become little people with opinions and their ways of being stubborn or sweet or kind or smart or tenderhearted or abrasive – we treasure their "becoming." They astonish us with what they say and do. We take pictures; we scrapbook, we write down memories, we celebrate the birthdays, the big events, the small events – we treasure it all. Dearly and deeply.

And Mary looked at her boy, Jesus, and did the same. In addition to treasuring she had found him again, perhaps seeing him teaching stirred a new realization for her as she began to catch glimpses of who Jesus was becoming.

She was raising him for this, of course. But it must have been bittersweet. We raise our children to get them to that point when they are ready to take wings and fly on their own. Mary was raising Jesus so he could grow up and do what he was born to do. Here he was, still her boy, but he was growing so fast. Oh, Mary, we know how that goes.

41-45 *Every year Jesus' parents traveled to Jerusalem for the Feast of Passover. When he was twelve years old, they went up as they always did for the Feast. When it was over and they left for home, the child Jesus stayed behind in Jerusalem, but his parents didn't know it. Thinking he was somewhere in the company of pilgrims, they journeyed for a whole day and then began looking for him among relatives and neighbors. When they didn't find him, they went back to Jerusalem looking for him.*

46-48 *The next day they found him in the Temple seated among the teachers, listening to them and asking questions. The teachers were all quite taken with him, impressed with the sharpness of his answers. But his parents were not impressed; they were upset and hurt.*

His mother said, "Young man, why have you done this to us? Your father and I have been half out of our minds looking for you."

49-50 He said, "Why were you looking for me? Didn't you know that I had to be here, dealing with the things of my Father?" But they had no idea what he was talking about. – Luke 2:41-50

Prayer: Dear God, as I teach and nurture the children in my life, help me give them roots and wings. In Jesus' name, I pray. Amen.

Reflect: Does it change your understanding and perspective of Jesus to think of him when he was growing up? What would you most like to know about Jesus' life from the years not recorded in Scripture?

Lom Stave Kirke
Oppland County, Norway

Norse

The nights were so quiet there. Seven miles from one town, eight from another. Our closest neighbors were cows, coyotes, and wild hogs.

Texas was unexpected, and my husband and I still wonder at all the events that fell into place that ultimately brought us there. It was like this: I knew for quite some time I had completed my call in Colorado, so I began looking at other options. We intended to return to Minnesota, but when no doors opened, and my father died around the same time, I had an overwhelming feeling that time was going so fast and I needed to move on. It was right at this vortex in time that the church in Texas began calling. Initially, we thought a family trip to interview Texas in February would be interesting and pleasantly warm, nothing else. It would be a good "practice interview."

That narrative began to shift quickly as soon as we arrived. The potluck they threw the Sunday we were there was hands down the best potluck there has ever been in the history of potlucks. Macaroni and cheese! Fried chicken! Comfort food in every direction. Norwegian delicacies and down-home southern favorites. Perfection.

But it wasn't just the potluck. They were so infinitely proud of their church. They knew they were a diamond and they just needed a pastor who appreciated their shine. Sure, anyone could spot their quirks. They still used hymnals from the 1930's, had no internet, they were extremely off the beaten path, yet fully expected that just the right pastor would help them grow. Nevertheless, in short order I became enchanted with everything there that was so different from where we currently were: the warm weather, the southern accents, the immense quiet, and a smaller church where I could know everyone's name.

While all those things were intriguing, they weren't the deciding factors. I know the exact moment when my heart beckoned me to start packing:

after two full days of meeting with the call committee, preaching at the worship service, and eating meals with parishioners, we were about to enjoy a quiet evening as a family before flying home the next day. I realized I had picked up one of the church's hymnals after the service and put it in my bag with my Bible, so we decided we would go to a neighboring town for supper and drop off the hymnal on the way.

We pulled up to the church, and I got out to put the book back in the unlocked sanctuary. The sun was setting, and as I paused by the door of the church, although my children were asleep in the back seat of the car, I could picture them running on that vast church lawn, riding their bikes on that long, quiet driveway. I could see them growing and being nurtured by that loving congregation who made sure there would be plenty of macaroni and cheese and other great "kid food" at that potluck. In that moment, I felt something calling me there. Was it the Holy Spirit? Was it my own mothering heart? Was it just that I was sick of living in the city and longing to be in the country again?

It was all those things. And that's how we ended up moving to Texas for five great years.

The Texas sun nearly melted our Minnesota bones many times over. When I wanted to go running, I ran at night because it was cooler and I could run undisturbed along the long, thin driveway that snaked along the back of the church property. Back and forth I ran, from the church sign to the parsonage driveway. It was a fair distance from one end to the other, and I never minded the repetition of winding back and forth beside that red brick church with its' steeple stretching toward the sky, under cover of the cedars and live oaks. If the moon was bright enough, I ran around the perimeter of the cemetery. Round and round. Reverently so.

The rock fence, the moonlight shining on the gravestones, the scent of wild honeysuckle, the Texas sky so big and the stars so bright, there's no other way to say it except that it was pure loveliness. For years, I felt content and happy, captivated with everything: the white limestone gravel, the charming balcony in the church, the stillness, the silence, warm winter days, my children so little, my congregation so beloved, I often whispered "thank you" into the night air.

But the stillness and silence began to get deafening. I didn't want it to be so. I wanted the enchantment to thrive, but bit by bit, day by day, it became clear I wouldn't be able to stay there. Life was beckoning me onward. The Spirit, my Self, my family, my goals were pushing me elsewhere, onward. It would do no good to fight it.

Someone else would get to be the pastor there and even as I resigned, I knew part of me would miss it forever. I knew in my bones I needed to go, but I never doubted a sliver of my heart would stay right there.

It's been this way with each church I have served. I loved them through and through. I don't know how else to be a pastor. In fact, I do not think there is any other way to be a pastor.

If there are words of wisdom I would give to anyone going into ministry it would be something like this: don't expect it to be a job. Expect it to be your life. Yes, you absolutely must have a world outside your church, too, and nurture it well so that you have something that is yours and doesn't belong to your congregation. That is important – especially when church life is having a rough season.

But expect that your congregation's cares will become your cares, and they will affect you to your core. They will break your heart like no one else. They will lift you up like no one else. You will love them deeply and yet come to a point when you know you must leave them.

And you will wonder how you could ever possibly love another congregation even half as much. But somehow, you will. By God's grace, you will.

I've served four congregations, and I treasure each of them. They have filled me full as we have learned and struggled and laughed together, and they have also gifted me with nearly every gray hair I have. I sacrificed much for them, but they have given me so much more.

This is the push and pull of a pastor's life. I would not trade it for another.

And let the peace of Christ rule in your hearts, to which indeed you were called in one body. And be thankful. Let the word of Christ dwell in you richly, teaching and admonishing one another in all wisdom, singing psalms and hymns and spiritual songs, with thankfulness in your hearts to God. And whatever you do, in word or deed, do everything in the name of the Lord Jesus, giving thanks to God the Father through him. – Colossians 3:15-17

Prayer: Dear God, you have guided me faithfully on this journey of life. Thank you for all that has been and all that is yet to be. In Jesus name, I pray. Amen.

Reflect: What has been one of the least expected turns your life has taken so far? What made it so unexpected? Is there anything you would change about it?

Our Savior's Lutheran Church at Norse
Clifton, Texas

Ashes to Ashes

Many years have passed since the first time that I went back to the place where I grew up after the new owners bought it and took down all the old buildings that were the setting for most every memory from my childhood.

It was late afternoon as I turned the corner off highway 65 onto Lost School Road. As I rounded the corner, I caught my breath. Every time I had turned that corner my whole life the first thing I would see was a white, wooden garage at the top of the hill, about a quarter mile in the distance. The house was next to it, cloaked in trees. Standing off to the side was a light on a tall post – the light that mom would always make sure to leave on if we were coming home at night.

Now there was nothing there. My car crept down the road and finally to the driveway, up the hill and came to a stop right in front of where the house used to be.

I got out of the car and stood motionless. It was the oddest feeling: haunting and solemn and sad and empty. The sidewalk where my brother and I had played marbles, gone. The garage with the basketball hoop where I had played for hours, gone. The clothesline where we hung our clothes, the chicken coop where I raised the hens, the house where we had been a family, gone, gone, gone.

I thought strange things - wondering if the trees would remember us at least, or if it could be remotely possible that if people lived and loved and shared life together in a place that some essence of you could live on there even after all physical evidence showed otherwise.

I noticed that on one side of the apple trees which had been behind our house, the leaves were withered and brown. As I moved closer, I realized it had been from intense heat and I knew what happened. That's how they took down the house. They burned it, let the ashes descend into the basement below, and then they covered them up.

It had to be done, of course. The house was falling apart. The wiring was bad; there were bats and mice and all sorts of disrepair. It needed to be torn down.

It was good really. I knew that. Someone else would build a home or a cabin there. Someone else would make memories with children and grandchildren there. Someone else would go sit by the lake, watch the sunrise over the meadow, listen to the breeze through the branches of the poplars and see how the noontime sun could make their leaves glimmer like silver coins. All those things were so good. Life was going on.

So why did it feel so much like death?

Because of course, it was that as well. I bent down and scooped up some of the dirt beneath my feet mingled with the ashes of all that used to be. So much now reduced to dust.

I took some pictures before I left. There were the trees that mom and I planted in the front yard when I was twelve and the lilac bush we grew from a clipping taken from grandma's yard. I looked one more time down toward the valley where the deer pause to drink from the pond and up toward the hill where mom used to take us sledding. Scores of memories every direction I turned. It would always be this way here. I sighed and slipped back into my car and drove away.

We all have our stories of ashes, don't we? Mine, I think of a home that once existed that is now just a memory. Yours might be the ash and ruin you found your life in after poor choices made. They could be the ashes of dreams you had for a relationship or the ashes of the prayers you prayed that a cure would be found or the ashes of a loved one whose body finally gave up its spirit at the end of a long life. Ashes are the sign of something that once was – but no more. We sweep them up and toss them away, we bury them, scatter them, or store them and try to forget.

On Ash Wednesday, we are marked with them. We choose to be marked with this grimy sign of death and endings. Why do such a thing?

We do it because we need a reminder that it is only through death that there is the possibility of new life. We do it because it is only through the repentance of Ash Wednesday, this season of Lent, pondering the last days and words of our Lord Jesus, remembering his last supper he shared with his disciples on Maundy Thursday, and kneeling at the foot of the cross where he hung on Good Friday that we can fully experience the joy of the resurrection on Easter morning.

We do it because there is palpable reverence and meaning in the rituals of Ash Wednesday. We place ashes in the shape of a cross on the foreheads of the smallest children to the oldest adults in the church and say, *"remember you are dust, and to dust you will return."* Whenever I mark a baby with that cross, the words stick in my throat, and I have to push them out. Ashes are a sign of endings and the blackness of sin and death. It feels wrong to place them on the pale, smooth, perfect skin of an innocent baby. Yet, it is a somber remembrance that we are all born into a beautiful and busted world. All of us will experience the fleeting fragility of this life. All need grace upon grace, from God and from each other.

And so, on Ash Wednesday, we are marked with a sign of death and ruin and dive deep into the season of Lent. We emerge into the trust that somehow, in some mysterious way, God is taking the ashes of our lives and working to breathe new life into us. For now, and forever.

18 Do not remember the former things, or consider the things of old.
19 I am about to do a new thing; now it springs forth, do you not perceive it?I will make a way in the wilderness and rivers in the desert. - Isaiah 43:18-19 New Revised Standard Version (NRSV)

Prayer: Dear God, help me to believe in all that is still possible through You. In Jesus' name, I pray. Amen.

Reflect: Think of a time when you experienced an ending. What were joyful new beginnings that came out of that time?

First Lutheran Church
Audubon, Minnesota
(Layered with a photo of water shining on a nearby lake)

I'll See You Later

Late into the summer afternoon we laughed and talked. The children played tag on the grass, and their shadows grew longer as the grownups lingered over one more cup of punch, another cookie. It was the kind of afternoon we didn't want to end. Time together had become rare over the years, and we looked forward to this get-together of family and friends for a long time. The children were lined up, and pictures were taken. Good friends smiled at each other over picnic tables and observed the traces of time gone by on one another's faces.

The boys and I had a long drive ahead of us, so finally it was time to leave. Michelle, my best friend since the first day of kindergarten, who now lives in Boston, walked us to our car. Her four boys ran circles around my two boys and they roughhoused like old friends, even though they had all only met that week. For at least that moment it was how we had always thought it would be – her children and my children all good friends - just like us.

Michelle and I stood by the car. We talked about how good it was to see each other again, how we would make sure that it wouldn't be so long until the next time we got together.

Owen and Jesse hugged their new little friends goodbye, and I buckled them into the car seats. Michelle and I faced each other; she smiled and said, "I'll see you later." In that moment, I thought about the first time I saw her, with pigtails and freckles, playing with blocks in the corner of a classroom. I remembered walks on gravel roads, long talks about boys, and then us driving around town in her dad's big orange truck. A thousand memories in a split second as the late afternoon breeze brushed through her hair. I simply smiled back at her and said, "I'll see you later."

As I got into my car and headed west, the boys dozed off, and I thought about the day and my dear friend and how we never said "goodbye."

Thursday of Holy Week, Maundy Thursday as it is often called, is sadder to me than Good Friday, partly because I can't fully comprehend the horror and agony of the crucifixion, but also because I know how hard it can be to say "goodbye". As I think about the last supper, the last meal that Jesus ate with his disciples, I can only imagine the sadness around that table. I think about them wondering exactly what he meant as he kept saying "remember me". *"Remember me by eating this bread and drinking this wine."* I imagine dry throats trying to choke down pieces of bread, sips of wine. "What does he mean? He's leaving us? What does he mean? One of us will betray him?" What had it all meant if it only had to end this way? Did the moments the disciples and Jesus had spent together, and all he had taught them mean anything if it all was just ending?

It isn't difficult to wonder that ourselves when we teeter on the brink of goodbyes: when the illness has run its course, when a journey together has culminated and paths separate, when we find ourselves at that moment when the roads diverge and we face an ending. How do we make sense of all that has been shared? Do the long walks and talks, the laughter, tears and all the moments shared mean anything if they just end in a goodbye? Where do we find our hope and peace when we face endings?

Jesus gave us his answer to that question when he gathered with his disciples and said, *"My children, I will be with you only a little longer. You will look for me, and just as I told the Jews, so I tell you now: Where I am going, you cannot come. A new command I give you: Love one another. As I have loved you, so you must love one another. By this all will know that you are my disciples, if you love one another." (John 13:35)*

Why this talk about love right now? It was more than just a new commandment or some good advice for their future work together and as they went about their lives. It was more than just a way for people to recognize Christ's ideals still in alive in the disciples.

Remember the words of Saint Paul: *Love never fails. But where there are prophecies, they will cease; where there are tongues, they will be stilled; where there is knowledge, it will pass away. For we know in part and we prophesy in part, 1but when perfection comes, the imperfect disappears.*

When I was a child, I talked like a child, I thought like a child, I reasoned like a child. When I became a man, I put childish ways behind me. Now we see but a poor reflection as in a mirror; then we shall see face to face. Now I know in part; then I shall know fully, even as I am fully known. And now these three abide: faith, hope and love. But the greatest of these is love. (I Corinthians 13:8-13)

Faith, hope, and love "abide." That word "abide" is a beautiful word that we don't hear too often anymore but it means, to go on, to remain, to last, to stay. Love abides. Love remains.

Jesus was telling his disciples that by continuing to love one another and to love others, he would always be with them. The presence of love in our world means Christ's resurrecting, eternal presence remains. And do you know what this means for us in our relationships here on earth? It means that everything matters because even if we have put just the tiniest bit of love into a relationship, that relationship will have an eternal dimension because love abides. Love remains. Love goes on forever.

This is how we can put time and energy into our relationships here and now and know that while moments of separation may come, whether short or long, those do not last. Not even the ultimate separation of death. Many things do die when the last breath is drawn: broken bodies, sadness, strained relationships, misunderstandings or bitterness or hopelessness — all those things do die, but what lasts is Love. Goodbyes are not forever for people who believe in a resurrected Lord. Instead, we can say, "I'll see you later."

Easter morning is yet far away. There is a sad and bitter journey we need to yet take with our Lord. Jesus leaves the meal with his disciples to go to the garden of Gethsemane to pray in anguish, knowing there remains a cup that only he can drink. He sees his only friends have fallen asleep rather than staying awake with him in this bitter hour.

But one thing we can trust as darkness falls on our Lord, as the chief priests, the officers of the temple guard and the elders come for him, as the crowd shouts for his death and he carries his own means of execution to Golgotha. The whole way, through his sweat, tears, blood, and his cries, if you listen carefully you will hear him whispering to us – not goodbye, never goodbye. He whispers, "I will see you later."

34-35 *"Let me give you a new command: Love one another. In the same way I loved you, you love one another. This is how everyone will recognize that you are my disciples—when they see the love you have for each other."* – John 13:34-35

Prayer: Dear Lord, thank you for the grace and mystery of the cross. In Jesus name, I pray, Amen.

Reflect: What does resurrection mean to you? Why is Jesus' resurrection important to the Christian faith?

Cemetery Cross
Our Savior's Lutheran Church at Norse
Clifton, Texas

Maundy Thursday

In many ways, Maundy Thursday is the darkest night of the church year. One could say that Good Friday is darker and more solemn as it closes with Christ in the tomb, all hope lost – and yet, I would argue that it is Maundy Thursday when the darkness presses in most deeply.

In the quiet darkness of Maundy Thursday, we remember Jesus, vulnerable and sharing a final meal with his disciples. Here he is, knowing that the end was coming and that these events that would lead to his death were set in motion by someone from his inner circle. While on Good Friday we can imagine the crowd of strangers noisily shouting, "Crucify him," – somehow the shouts of an angry mob are easier to understand than the betrayal of a friend, a loved one. The torture he endured on Friday was horrible, but the cruelest blow was that of the kiss of his friend, Judas.

Have you ever betrayed someone you love? Whether on purpose or by accident? Have you caused harm to another?

If you have, you know that there are the stories we don't like to tell. These are memories that haunt and stories we shove deep inside. We put on a smile and pretend they don't exist. We can drown them with drink or soften their edges with pills and yet, they remain. Their truth cannot be dimmed.

My mom went through a time of significant depression, and that was why she came from Minnesota to live with us in Texas the last six months of her life. Her sadness was so overpowering that she no longer made an effort to eat or take her medicine or do anything without someone to make sure she did so. We hoped that some warm weather and being with family would boost her spirits in time.

When mom agreed to come and stay with us, I was so glad. The ways that she lovingly cared for my brother and me when we were growing up, and took care of my dad during his many years of poor health, I wanted to extend that same kind of care to her when she needed it. I missed her so much in all the years we lived far away. She agreed to come to Texas when I brought up the idea, but right before we left her house for the last time she said, "I don't think I should go." But everything had already been planned and it was supposed to be just for a while until she felt better, so I said, "It's okay, mom. I want you to come." I never dreamed that she would never return, otherwise I would have let her have time to say 'goodbye.' I would have thought less about what I wanted as her daughter, and what she wanted and needed as a person. As it was, she wearily turned and got in the car, and we left her hometown for the last time.

We moved her into a room in our house. Her anxiety and depression were so deep that her days were mostly spent sitting at the kitchen table, hardly speaking. Each day, I made her breakfast and went to work, came home and made her lunch, then back to work for a few more hours until I came home to make her supper. Immediately after supper, she quietly stood up and went to her room to go to bed. There was none of her former good cheer or joy in life. Three days a week, I took her to a support group for seniors who were going through severe depression. At the same time, the boys were busy with preschool, and my final project for my doctorate was reaching its' deadline.

I took mom to doctor's appointments and checked her blood sugar twice a day. She had diabetes, liver troubles and a heart condition that required every month she get the thickness of her blood checked so she wouldn't get clots. These were all things that she tended to before this, but now that she couldn't, I was determined to take care of all of it for her.

And after a while, it felt like we were finding our way. It seemed like the support group was helping mom and now and then I saw glimpses of her old self. I was getting my work done, finishing my dissertation, and getting the boys and mom where they needed to be. It was a blur of days, and I wasn't sleeping much, but it felt like everything was going to be okay.

Then one afternoon I noticed mom was shaky, and she went to lie down in her room. I went to check on her, and I saw she had thrown up, was disoriented and couldn't speak. We called the ambulance, and she went to the ER in Waco. In the emergency room, the doctor was inquiring about her medications, and asking when was the last time she had her blood checked.

You see, mom just had a stroke because a clot developed in her heart. A perfectly round clot the size of a walnut. And the clot was there because her blood had gotten too thick. And her blood had gotten too thick because her medication dosage was apparently not right anymore. And her medication dosage was not right because, as I ticked back through the days and weeks in my mind, I realized it had been well over six weeks since we had it checked, instead of one month as it was supposed to be.

Because of that clot, mom had to have surgery to get it removed. She never recovered, and died a few months later.

I used to joke about my forgetfulness, how I write everything down to remember both small and big things. I figured if being forgetful was my worst flaw, then it wasn't so bad. But in all my juggling of life and family and work and school, I forgot an astronomically important thing – to make sure she got her blood checked every month without fail – and the consequences were catastrophic.

Even though I would never, ever have intentionally betrayed or harmed my mom, I did. She needed me to watch out for her, to take care of all that she no longer could, and I blew it. Utterly and entirely blew it. There are no words to express the sorrow I feel about this.

All I can do is confess it. God and I have talked about it an awful lot over the years. As I proclaim the forgiveness of sins each week, I remind myself that forgiveness extends to me, too. One of these days I will believe it.

I have told this story only a few times, and the first was on a Maundy Thursday. I shared it in a hushed sanctuary, shortly before we left Texas to come to Minnesota. I told it because I needed to tell it, but maybe also because I wanted to leave part of it there. I wanted to stop carrying around the full weight of that memory and I imagined my only chance at that was to let the light of day hit it.

I also wanted to say it out loud because I suspected each person in that sanctuary would understand in their own way. I was right, because more than a few of them stopped by in the days that followed to tell me their own stories and sadnesses they have been carrying around.

Although our faults and failures may be different, we have histories and secrets, regrets and sins. We may do a great job of hiding all these things so that no one would guess how broken we are inside, but we know. And God knows. And when we share in Holy Communion, we remember that even so, we are loved. We are treasured. It was because of our brokenness that Jesus sacrificed all for us. Even though nothing can erase our brokenness, or fix all our mistakes, God is able to always, somehow, still use us for good.

It seems too good to be true. Judas couldn't imagine it. He was so overwhelmed by what he had done that first he went and tried to give back the thirty pieces of silver he received for betraying Jesus. After that, he immediately went and hanged himself. He couldn't bear the thought of what he had done.

Human beings feel the need to hoard guilt and shame – not God. Judas couldn't forgive himself, but Jesus could. He did. On Maundy Thursday we remember how Jesus the Christ knelt and washed the feet of his disciples, even Judas. He begged them to love one another, even as his heart grieved knowing how they would fail. He loved them through his tears, even Judas. His forgiveness was so great that the cross would not extinguish it. His forgiveness is so great that it was for everyone for all time, even Judas. Even you. Even me.

7-10 Because of the sacrifice of the Messiah, his blood poured out on the altar of the Cross, we're a free people—free of penalties and punishments chalked up by all our misdeeds. And not just barely free, either. Abundantly free! - Ephesians 1:7-9 The Message (MSG)

Prayer: Dear God, thank you for forgiving us even when we can't forgive ourselves. In Jesus name, I pray. Amen.

Reflect: Why do you think it can be easier to forgive others than to forgive ourselves?

Good Shepherd Cemetery
Henning, Minnesota

Pouring Out Love

The sense of smell can bring back memories in such powerful ways. I have what was left of my father's aftershave. I keep it in my dresser and now and then when I come across it, I'll open it, close my eyes and sniff. I'm instantly brought back to when he would take my face in his hands after he was done shaving and pat some of the good smelling aftershave on my face, too. The smell of wood smoke brings me back to summer nights on the shores of Lake Carlos when I was a camp counselor. The scent of lilacs transports my thoughts directly to my grandmother's yard.

And if we were living in the moment of the encounter between Mary of Bethany and Jesus shortly before he was betrayed, the room would be filled with the scent of pure nard, an intensely aromatic, thick, amber-colored oil. We don't know how many people are there, but we do know Mary comes in with this oil, and begins to anoint and massage Jesus' feet.

As if this scene weren't tender enough, she then uses her hair to gently wipe off his feet. This scene is scandalous. She loosens her hair in a room full of men, an honorable woman never did that. An honorable woman only let her hair down in the presence of her husband.

She pours perfume on Jesus' feet, which was also not done. The head, maybe, as people did that to kings, but not the feet. Then she touches him. A single woman rubbing a single man's feet was never done, not even among closest friends. She then wipes the perfume off with her hair.

It is a scene of complete generosity and extravagant affection. This oil was extremely expensive, worth about a year's salary at the time. To use this oil so lavishly and all on one person seems foolish at first glance. Judas Iscariot voices the concern that others in the room are thinking, "Why wasn't this oil sold and the money given to the poor?"

Judas seems right on the mark, in fact, he seems to be saying something that Jesus himself would say. Jesus was always a champion for the poor and the oppressed, but here he defends Mary and says, *"No, leave her alone. You'll always have the poor with you, but you won't always have me." (– John 12:7)*

What was this? Was Jesus, who used every moment as a teaching moment, teaching them even now and reminding them he was the lamb, the ultimate sacrifice? Or did he merely want to treasure for a moment the fragrance of the oils filling the room, the touch of a friend offering him comfort? Did he want to savor these small pleasures before the next things were fulfilled?

The whole story is achingly sad and bittersweet. We can guess how precious those final moments with friends must have been for Jesus. Did Mary's kindness and care for him bring him some measure of comfort as he endured all that happened in the next days? Did the scent of the oils linger on his skin even as he was brought before Pilate? Did the memory of gentle hands lovingly massaging his feet have enough power to lessen some of the blows that other hands soon dealt?

While this scripture raises many questions, the actions of Mary are not mysterious to me. She reminds me of when Peter wanted to make those dwelling places on the mountaintop the day of Jesus' transfiguration. Peter wanted to stay in that moment of wonder forever. His actions and words often interpreted as brash and even foolish, but who doesn't say and do impetuous things when wonder and joy have filled you to the top? And the people around Mary might shake their heads at her foolishness of sharing all that precious oil with just one person. They might tsk tsk at her unrestrained actions as she kneels at Jesus' feet and even lets down her hair to use it as a towel, but these were the things she had to give. Who doesn't understand that feeling of wanting to give all that we have for the people who mean the most to us? We'd give anything to see them not suffer or be harmed. If we know the end is near, we do everything we can to make that end pain-free, dignified, as meaningful as possible, and surround that person with love.

What Mary had to give were these precious oils and her actions. She shared all of it without holding back because soon she would no longer have Jesus near to give him all that she could give. She had to give it all and give it then. This was no time for stingy love or small gifts, this was a time to pour it all out because soon, there would be no more time.

She did it for Jesus, but she was also doing it for herself. That's how giving is, we need to do it. Generosity never leaves us empty, wanting or poorer for having done it; it only helps fill the empty places and gives wholeness to our brokenness.

I've heard Mary described as a prophet, that with her actions here and using these precious oils she's not only preparing Jesus for burial but she is showing the extravagance of God's love.

In fact, some call Mary "the prodigal woman." One of the meanings of the word "prodigal" is "extravagant." Throughout Christian history we have focused on its other meaning, "wasteful" – as in the prodigal son took his inheritance and wasted it. But when we look at that word "prodigal" knowing its other definitions we see prodigal happenings all over the place in our scriptures. The prodigal father who welcomed back the son and gave him a robe and a meal and his place in the home, loving him extravagantly even though he did not deserve it. The prodigal shepherd who loses one sheep and will not rest, goes over the top in his searching, until that lost sheep is found. The prodigal widow who only has two small copper coins and she recklessly gives them both away trusting that little becomes much when it is placed in the master's hands. The prodigal woman, Mary, pouring out oil and tears, letting down her hair and her guard to love profusely. The prodigal God, Jesus, making his way down the Via Dolorosa and ultimately giving up his very life, loving us with everything he has, then and now and forever.

When we begin to take note of this Spirit of generosity that fills our Holy Scriptures it is easy to see why the happiest people are those who have learned how to give.

Let's take a lesson from Mary of Bethany.

We begin by giving of what we have. As she poured out expensive oils without thought of the cost, we give generously as well, and if that is hard to do, which it is for most of us, we work bit by bit to become better at it. We try to loosen our grip on stuff; loosen our worries about money and materials and instead see all that has been entrusted to us as means to bless others. Anyone who is wise knows that anything we think is ours isn't really ours, it's a gift from God given to us for a time and to be shared - our view of the world becomes more beautiful when we see everything this way. Worries become less as we take our focus off our wants and instead minister to the needs of others. Our time becomes more meaningful when we use it to benefit others rather than solely for our entertainment and comfort.

Giving is a joyful thing, it lightens our load in so many ways. Giving frees us from much we never really needed anyway and opens the doors and windows wide for things like peace and joy and love to rush in.

One night during seminary, I was sitting at supper with a group of friends. One of my friends, Emily, said to my other friend, Steve, "Hey, I like your sweater." Steve immediately took off his sweater and gave it to her. Emily exclaimed, "no, don't give it to me! I was just saying I like it!" But Steve insisted. He smiled and told us he had been practicing his giving. He made a promise to himself that if anyone said they liked something he had, if possible, he was going to give it away to remind himself how little he needed. He said that ever since he started doing it, he felt better and happier. He said, "Please, as a favor to me, take the sweater!" Emily laughed and took the sweater. She said to him, "you are nuts."

I think of that night at the supper table and how Steve was so willing and even joyful to let go of his stuff, to walk home on a chilly night with no sweater. He knew he didn't need it. He recognized how practicing generosity opened up a good space inside him.

We may not have precious oils or long hair to let down to wipe Jesus' feet, yet we can still ask ourselves each day what kind of fragrant offering we can give to show how very much we love him, how thankful we are for this life and our blessings. Each day we can be the prodigal son or daughter, too. We can love, live, help and give extravagantly.

1-3 Six days before Passover, Jesus entered Bethany where Lazarus, so recently raised from the dead, was living. Lazarus and his sisters invited Jesus to dinner at their home. Martha served. Lazarus was one of those sitting at the table with them. Mary came in with a jar of very expensive aromatic oils, anointed and massaged Jesus' feet, and then wiped them with her hair. The fragrance of the oils filled the house.4-6 Judas Iscariot, one of his disciples, even then getting ready to betray him, said, "Why wasn't this oil sold and the money given to the poor? It would have easily brought three hundred silver pieces." He said this not because he cared two cents about the poor but because he was a thief. He was in charge of their common funds, but also embezzled them.7-8 Jesus said, "Let her alone. She's anticipating and honoring the day of my burial. You always have the poor with you. You don't always have me." - John 12:1-8

Dear God, help me give generously of my time, energy, and resources. In Jesus' name, I pray. Amen.

Reflect: What have been your most joyful experiences with giving? Can you think of a time you regretted being generous? If so, why?

**Richwood Lutheran Church
Calloway, Minnesota**

Frances

I found out yesterday that a friend of mine in Texas died. It wasn't a surprise as she was ninety-five years old and pneumonia set in a few days ago. Her name was Frances, and she was a member of my church in Texas. Her husband had been a pastor, and together they were missionaries in Japan for decades. She lived in many places and parsonages during her life, and we were kindred spirits in countless ways, regardless of our age difference.

When mom died, Frances was a comforting, mothering presence. I loved to sit in her nursing home room, and we worked on crossword puzzles together or just talked. My boys brought her handfuls of flowers they picked for her, and she grand-mothered them, exclaiming over them and making them feel special and loved, as children ought to feel.

It was agonizing for us to say "goodbye" to her when we moved away from Texas, but she understood how we longed to be back in our home state. When we left, I knew I would likely never see her again here on earth, and now I know this is true.

So, while I'm physically here in my office in Minnesota, my mind is drifting back to Texas today, and thinking about how her memorial service will be. Someone will climb up the steep stairs into the old balcony and ring the bell ninety-five times, once for each year of her life, as she is brought from the church out to the quiet cemetery to be laid to rest next to her husband's grave. The church ladies will make a lunch for the family. Then, one by one, the parking lot will empty out.

Earth to earth, ashes to ashes, dust to dust.

Each time I say those words at a graveside service, they feel like sadness and endings, but my heart understands they are so much more than that. They aren't the end of the story. With each dear parishioner, each friend I have buried, I remind my congregations and myself again and again that there are no final goodbyes when our hope is in Jesus, the one who defeated death and the grave. There's a healing, a wholeness, a hope that we only catch glimpses of here, but someday it will be revealed when we are all reunited in the presence of the One who made us.

Nothing changes the aching truth that it's hard to let go, to realize a chapter has ended, to know there will never again be those talks, those crossword puzzles.

But in the meantime, I give thanks to God for Frances and so many others, and I hold on tight with both hands to Jesus' promise.

The promise of Easter.

51 Lo! I tell you a mystery. We shall not all sleep, but we shall all be changed, 52 in a moment, in the twinkling of an eye, at the last trumpet. For the trumpet will sound, and the dead will be raised imperishable, and we shall be changed. 53 For this perishable nature must put on the imperishable, and this mortal nature must put on immortality. 54 When the perishable puts on the imperishable, and the mortal puts on immortality, then shall come to pass the saying that is written:

"Death is swallowed up in victory."
55 "O death, where is thy victory?
O death, where is thy sting?" – I Corinthians 15:51-55 NRSV

Prayer: Dear God, thank you for the promise of the resurrection. In Jesus name, I pray. Amen.

Reflect: What does Easter mean to you? Has its significance changed for you over the course of your life?

Saron (Hamden) Lutheran Cemetery
Audubon, Minnesota

A Baccalaureate Message

Lately, making rounds on the internet are college graduation speeches being given across the country. Various celebrities and people who have made their mark in one way or another are being asked to share a few words of wisdom with graduating students to give them some food for thought as they step out into the future. These speeches often have a similar but compelling tone: they begin with a story of some hardship or challenge the presenter had to endure or overcome and the process of how they made it through that difficulty. Then, the speaker offers words of encouragement or tips for how the listeners can and must find ways to persevere through the challenges in their own lives.

Commencement speeches are plum full of inspiring quotes – here are some examples:

"It doesn't matter how far you might rise. At some point, you are bound to stumble. And when you do I want you to know this, remember this: There is no such thing as failure. Failure is just life trying to move us in another direction." – Oprah Winfrey in a speech to Harvard

"Death is very likely the single best invention of life. It's life's change agent; it clears out the old to make way for the new. Right now, the new is you. But someday, not too long from now, you will gradually become the old and be cleared away. Sorry to be so dramatic, but it's quite true. Your time is limited, so don't waste it living someone else's life." – Steve Jobs in a speech at Stanford

"And now go, and make interesting mistakes, make amazing mistakes, make glorious and fantastic mistakes. Break rules. Leave the world more interesting for your being here." – Neil Gaiman in a speech at the University of the Arts

Commencement speeches can be powerful and memorable because they are given at a time of great transition, a place in life all of us will experience, again and again, a time when the listeners are teetering between all that has been completed and all that is yet to come.

In the gospel according to Saint John, Jesus gives his own commencement speech of sorts. Although there are no caps and gowns and no diplomas, it is a time of great transition. He is talking to his disciples on the night he will soon be arrested and taken away to be killed. He has much to share with them. He is telling the disciples to continue to live and serve in his name even though he wasn't going to be with them in the same way any longer, he encourages obedience to his commandments and speaks of the Spirit who will be with them forever. (John 14:15-17)

In Greek, the word for the Holy Spirit is "paraclete" which can also be interpreted as Advocate or Friend or Helper, Encourager, Comforter.

The Holy Spirit is with us always, promising to intercede for us with sighs too deep for words to express, helping us suspect there might yet be hope when everything else might be pointing toward desolation, calling us, shaping us, shifting us, inspiring us. And just as that Holy Spirit is with us always, it affects the way that we are present in the lives of others as well.

For whom in your life are you their paraclete? Who are your paracletes? Who are those people who have been there for you – helping, encouraging, comforting you on the journey? We need these paracletes in our lives: friends, family, and mentors. These people who walk alongside us in our daily living.

The well-known comedic actor and Saturday Night Live alumnus, Will Ferrell, gave the commencement address at his alma mater, The University of Southern California, in 2017 and he told a beautiful story of how his career found its seeds right there on that campus. He said he graduated from college with a degree in Sports Information and immediately moved right back home for two solid years. He thanked his mom who was in the audience as he gave the speech. He said, "she recognized that while I had an interest in pursuing sportscasting, my gut was telling me that I really wanted to pursue something else. And that something else was comedy."

He went on to talk about how the campus became his testing lab and theater. He was always trying to make his friends laugh. He said, "I had a work-study job at the humanities audiovisual department that would allow me to take off from time to time. By allow me, I mean I would just leave and they didn't notice." If Ferrell he knew his friends were attending class close by, he would leave his job and crash a lecture in costume and character. One day a friend told him he should crash his literature class and so Ferrell put together a janitor's outfit complete with work gloves, safety goggles, a dangling lit cigarette, and a bucket full of cleaning supplies. He then walked into the class, interrupting the lecture, informing the professor that he'd just been sent from Physical Plant to clean up a student's vomit.

A month later, the professor of that class, a distinguished professor named Ronald Gottesman, grabbed Ferrell by the shoulder when he was walking through campus. Ferrell said he was sure that he was going to tell him never to do that again. Instead, he told him that he loved him barging in on his class, that it was one of the funniest things he had ever seen, and would he please do it again?

So, on invitation from Professor Gottesman Ferrell continued to barge in on his lecture class from time to time in full character as 'the guy from Physical Plant' coming by to check on things, and the professor would joyfully play along.

Ferrell said, "One time I got my hands on a power drill, and I just stood outside the classroom door operating the drill for a good minute. Unbeknownst to me, Professor Gottesman was wondering aloud to his class, 'I wonder if we're about to get a visit from our Physical Plant guy?' I then walked in as if on cue and the whole class erupted in laughter. After leaving, Professor Gottesman then weaved the surprise visit into his lecture on Walt Whitman and the *Leaves of Grass*. Moments like these encouraged me to think maybe I was funny to whole groups of people who didn't know me, and this wonderful professor had no idea how his encouragement of me — to come and interrupt his class no less — was enough to give myself permission to be silly and weird."

I loved that story and how that teacher found a way to be encouraging to Will Ferrell, letting him use his classroom as a lab to test out his comedic talents. The teacher could have been so wrapped up in himself, the material he wanted to present, and the brief amount of time he had to teach it, and gotten upset that Ferrell interrupted, but instead, he saw a young guy with talent and an opportunity for joy to be shared. You can't schedule that. You can only be open to it and encourage it when you spot it.

It might seem a bit odd to think of this as a holy thing and yet we get to participate in the work of the Holy Spirit when we are encouragers, when we are comforters and helpers. This is no small thing. It changes lives. It directs courses and pathways, and even if we accomplish many great things in our lives, this work of encouragement is among the most important work any of us will ever get to do.

So, my dear graduates, you have hopefully had many encouragers who have loved you and supported you and gotten you to this exciting time in your journey. I pray that as you move forward through the days and months and years to come, you will remember to pay it forward. Every day, look for ways to encourage those around you. Think about uplifting words to say. Work hard to be the one who helps joyfully, who serves happily, encourages abundantly. May you, and all of us, excel at this Holy Work in Jesus' name. God bless you always. Amen.

15-17 *"If you love me, show it by doing what I've told you. I will talk to the Father, and he'll provide you another Friend so that you will always have someone with you. This Friend is the Spirit of Truth. You know him already because he has been staying with you, and will even be in you! - John 14:15-17 (MSG)*

Prayer: Dear God, open my eyes to see someone who could use an encouraging word today. In Jesus' name, I pray. Amen.

Reflect: Who have been your encouragers along the way? How did they affect your life? Have you thanked them?

Folden Lutheran Church
Vining, Minnesota
(Layered with photo of sun and clouds)

The Closing of the Sanctuary

"With thanks to God for the work accomplished in this place, I declare this sanctuary to be vacated for the purposes of Good Shepherd Lutheran Church, in the name of the Father, and of the Son, and of the Holy Spirit...."

The summer of 2016, I attended the final service in the sanctuary where I went to church the whole time I was growing up. Now, that sanctuary has been torn down and a new worship structure has been built.

I was glad to be invited back to participate in the service along with other pastors who grew up there and served there. It was important to me to go because I love that place and I am happy to be a daughter of that congregation. I also wanted my kids to have another memory there aside from their memories of the funerals of their grandparents. I wanted to one more time look out into that sanctuary and picture my mother there, where she always sat. I wanted to again see the pastors who meant so much to my family and me.

I've never been a part of a service like that before. To think that no more church bulletins would be assembled in the secretary's office where my mom once worked, no more sermons would be written in the same old pastor's office, no more children would run up to the balcony to peer down at the happenings below, not another hymn or scripture or prayer would be uttered under that roof, it was as strange a feeling to be there as I imagined it would be.

The pastor's voice cracked as he did the closing rite. I was glad because that's how we all felt: trusting that in the end, all would be well, but for now our hearts overflowing with retrospection and melancholy.

I was asked to give a brief reflection during the service. This was what I said:

"Like you, at a time like this, I can't help but think about the memories cradled within these walls. Some of my very earliest memories took place right here, sitting next to my grandmother. She often teared up at some point during the service and pulled a tissue out of her sleeve or out of her brassiere and dabbed at her eyes. She taught me about the beauty of preparedness as she always had a tissue on her somewhere. It was here I began to appreciate how fun and good it is to sing together as Mrs. Guse taught us songs. I received my first assertiveness training right here in the front row as my friend, Joni, demonstrated how to talk back to older brothers and their friends. Confirmation day in 1985, I wore brand new high heels with little bows. I could barely walk in those tall heels but I loved them even as they sunk into the spring grass of the church lawn as our class picture was taken.

Pastor Vetter asked me to preach one summer Sunday when I was in college. I remember walking up to the front in my pale pink suit, petrified. I think my mom was even more nervous than I was and I couldn't understand that until I became a mom, too. I was ordained right here in 1999, and this congregation celebrated with me and prayed for me. I wore my brown suit with a tiger-striped scarf.

In 2007 we brought our son, Jesse here to be baptized. Pastor Johnson led the whole baptismal rite and let me put that Spirit-flooded water on my baby's head in the name of the Father, and of the Son, and of the Holy Spirit. Not long after that, he let me sprinkle the sand on my dad's casket at the graveside service, and then at mom's the next year. I wore my long black skirt and my red and black jacket with a black scarf. It was November.

No matter where life has brought me or how many years have gone by, the story of my history feels knit into this place. No matter what was happening or what was on my mind or what I chose to wear, here I was clothed with the love of Jesus, gifted in his grace again and again. Of all the things I learned here, this is the blessed sum of it. I am so glad – glad for all that God has done here and all that God is yet to do. In Jesus' name."

After that worship service and a morning of thinking about endings, my boys and I picked up my mom's friend, Norma, and we went out to the piece of land where I grew up. My brother and I sold that property to her son and his wife. Ever since, they have been busy tearing down the old, shabby buildings and building a beautiful new home and landscaping and gorgeous trails throughout the woods we loved to explore when we were kids.

Enough years have passed that it is no longer painful to be out there and think of all that has been lost from our childhood and how we miss our parents. Now, I can look at how beautiful they have made the place, and I think, "Mom and Dad would have thought this was pretty great." It is good to see new life there and new memories being made. Only one of the old apple trees behind our house remains, but new ones have sprung up all around the property. The lilac bush mom planted from clippings from Grandma's lilac bush still blooms. They have planted lovely wildflowers in the fields and new young trees, but the evergreen mom and I planted still towers over the lawn, healthy and strong. So much is new there, but traces of my family remain.

A pastor friend told me a story about a burial service where at the end, the family released balloons into the air. They were white balloons with white strings. As they floated up, up, up, in one large group, bending and twisting with the wind into the blue summer sky, she said, "they looked like a large group of sperm heading up into the air." We laughed hard, and then I said, "But it's kind of symbolic, isn't it? New life happens all the time! Right there, at the end of the graveside service, little swimmers still making their way." We laughed some more.

New life happens all the time. God makes it so. Most of the time it just happens through endings first, that's the hard part.

For everything there is a season, and a time for every matter under heaven. – Ecclesiastes 3:1

Have I not commanded you? Be strong and courageous. Do not be frightened, and do not be dismayed, for the Lord your God is with you wherever you go." – Joshua 1:9

Prayer: Dear God, give us bravery in our beginnings and peace in our endings. In Jesus' name, I pray. Amen.

Reflect: Are there significant places in your life that no longer exist? A childhood home? A former church? A school? How did you feel when you knew the place was being torn down or renovated into something else? What makes a place more than just boards and nails, and a location on the map?

The former sanctuary of Good Shepherd Lutheran Church
Henning, Minnesota

Love One Another

A few nights before my wedding, some friends and I spent a few hours gluing hundreds of tiny pieces of paper to hundreds of Hershey's kisses. They were little party favors that would be placed at each table during the reception. Printed on the pieces of paper were quotes about love. Everyone had a different one. I had so much fun finding all those quotes. There were thought-provoking quotes like one of my favorites from Toni Morrison when she said, "I didn't fall in love, I rose in it." There were cute ones like from Winnie the Pooh, "It isn't much good having anything exciting like floods if you can't share them with someone." There were words from the poets, "who, being loved, is poor?" (Oscar Wilde) and great leaders, "my greatest good fortune in a life of brilliant experiences has been to find you, and to lead my life with you." (Winston Churchill to his wife)

As I found these quotes, typed them up, and then cut them into slips of paper before my friends came over with hot glue guns in hand, it was a blessing to think about those words. To think about reflections of love, some romantic, some cute, some bittersweet, some courageous, and to think about the love I had come to know in my own life.

Chad and I weren't engaged very long. It was an evening in late April when he asked me to marry him as we sat talking at my kitchen table. We decided we'd get married at the end of July. The weeks and months that followed seemed to bask in a long, sweet glow of goodness. That summer the weather was always perfect, every meal was the best meal, every song that came on the radio was one of my favorites, and everything overflowed with joy. I was living in the first bloom of love, and love has many seasons, so I was determined to enjoy every minute of those quick days.

We are seventeen years, two children, and thousands of miles from that summer now. While I'm thankful for those first weeks and months of love's first bloom, I'm more grateful for the time that has passed since then. The sharing of life. In my mind, it is a slide-show of moments: loading a moving van in New York, buying our first house in Colorado, holding our boys after they were born, standing by the graves of Chad's parents and then my parents, loading a moving van again and seeing the mountains disappear in the rear-view mirror and arriving in Texas, then a few years later in Minnesota. The seasons of our lives and the lives of the people we love unfolding all around us.

But that is how love is, isn't it? Some bits of it are about the romantic quotes, the sweet kisses, love's first breathless bloom. But true love is something different. True love is what remains after the first bloom fades. True love is the companionship through good times and bad. True love is steady. True love is built over a lifetime, only recognized through shared experience and achieving shared goals and continuing to choose each other, to care about the other's cares, to listen to stories you've heard before. It is continuing to build onto the village you've begun rather than leaving to start a new one. I think C.S. Lewis said it best when he said, *"Being in love is a good thing, but it is not the best thing. Love...is a deep unity maintained by the will and deliberately strengthened by habits reinforced by the grace which both partners ask and receive from God...On this love the engine of marriage is run; being in love was the explosion that started it."*

Jesus talks about love and says that love is not just a nice thing, it is something we are commanded to do. Jesus says, *"This is my commandment, that you love one another as I have loved you."* (John 13:34)

It is a big commandment because he doesn't just mean those people whom we have vowed to love, our partners and children, but to have real love for everyone we encounter.

What does this mean?

It means that everyone: you and me, and the college kids jogging down Cascade Avenue, the homeless folks at the bus terminal, the person driving too slow in front of you, that stranger on the sidewalk, and the one sitting next to you at jury duty, everyone we meet, in fact, has unsurpassable worth. Everyone we meet, according to Jesus, is worth our time, and so precious that Jesus died so that they could have a chance to live and breathe and love.

And so, God beckons us to treat each other with grace and goodness; to go out of our way to help, to risk our intricate schedules and let go of some of our fears and try to be the change we wish to see in this world. Because when we do, we begin to understand love.

I believe one of the reasons God has given me children is so that I will learn something about this. I've learned I can't get too worked up about time or about getting where I need to be too quickly when my children are with me. This was especially true when they were very little.

It was one of those days that happen now and then when you have a baby and a toddler. Our baby, Jesse, had woken up at four a.m. crying. Wintery roads, a day of meetings, and a stunning headache had frayed my nerves. Soon, I could pick up my children from the church nursery and go home.

The phone rang, it was a parishioner calling to tell me her father was in the hospital. I said I would go see him that night, but inside I was nearly crying. I was so tired. Motherhood and Pastor-hood were both such blessings, but my blessings were exhausting me.

I decided to bring my toddler, Owen, with me to the hospital. He was used to accompanying me on visits like this and he often brought a measure of cheer into the hospital room that I alone don't bring. We visited the fellow, Owen bowing little his head and joining in on the prayer I said, and then as we were leaving Owen pulled me toward the cafeteria. He asked for some string cheese and I told him to find a table.

In a sea of empty tables, Owen plopped down at the one table that already had someone sitting at it. The silver-haired woman smiled at him with amusement over her cup of coffee. My heart sighed, the last thing I wanted to do was make small talk with a stranger. I just wanted Owen to eat his cheese and then we could get home.

I joined them at the table and Owen ate his cheese. The woman and I talked, and after a bit, she told me she was at the hospital because her daughter was dying. She clutched a tissue in her hand but she looked like she was too tired to cry anymore. She didn't know I am a pastor, but still, she poured out her grief and pain to us. I listened, and I knew the moment was holy because Owen, who was almost always moving, didn't move a muscle. He just sat there eating his cheese and considering the woman with his big blue eyes.

After a long while, she said she had to go. She reached out and touched Owen's hand and said, "He's precious." I smiled.

As we drove home that night, I was still tired. It had still been a long day. Yet, I knew I had received a blessing. In a hospital cafeteria, on a winter evening, my little son and a woman I did not know reminded me how beautiful and brief this life is. I was thankful my dear boy decided to sit at that table, forcing me to interact with a stranger and get out of my own head. Children often point out to us what we are too busy or too blind to see ourselves.

Love. It's about learning how to really see each other - and not turning away once we do. It's about slowing down so that we have time for each other.

How might you be better at loving your partner?
How might you be better at loving your children?
How might you be better at loving your co-workers?
How might you be better at loving the strangers you meet?
These are questions we all need to consider – but because Jesus is asking them of us all.

"Let me give you a new command: Love one another. In the same way I loved you, you love one another. This is how everyone will recognize that you are my disciples—when they see the love you have for each other." - John 13:34-35 The Message

Prayer: Dear God, help me love all the people you have brought to my life. In Jesus name, I pray. Amen.

Reflect: What is one way you could intentionally be more loving today?

The abandoned Saron (Hamden) Lutheran Church
Building relocated to Detroit Lakes, Minnesota

Jewelry Box

The music box stopped working. It no longer makes a sound.

My mom did not have a lot of fancy things. She and dad lived very simply, partly out of necessity since Dad couldn't work for most of his adult life due to his disability, but also because of fierce thriftiness. If they could make something keep working, keep serving its' purpose, no matter how bad it looked or how many times it had to be taped together, they kept using it.

Among the things I found in mom's house after she died were piles of notebooks in which she had recorded every purchase, bill paid, and offering to the church over the last fifty-two years.

Every penny mattered. They didn't say things like "it's just twenty bucks, why not get it?" They said things like, "waste not, want not," and "don't throw that (name of item) away, we'll just duct tape it together. Good as new!"

The window in my upstairs bedroom (which had a beautiful view of the hills and woods in the distance) broke when I was in high school and rather than get a new window, my dad asked my brother to nail a board over it. The fact that my room was now a dark tomb with no natural light was not a consideration.

The car we had when my brother and I were small could only be started by inserting a screwdriver somewhere in the engine. Rather than fix whatever was causing this, mom and dad drove it that way for years.

I suspect I don't comprehend how tight finances were for my parents. When dad was forced to retire from ministry due to his health, he received a small disability pension each month, but it was very minimal. It was small enough that we still qualified to receive government cheese, rice, and food stamps. Mom couldn't work because dad wasn't well enough to take care of us kids, plus he needed her to care for him as well.

So, we "made do."

For however little material possessions mom wanted or needed during her life, it became even more this way the last year of her life. When she came to live with us in Texas, I ached to be able to ease the sadness she was carrying. Since I didn't know what else to do – I brought her little "treats" – things that she would usually have enjoyed: some scented soap or a pretty cup, fresh stationery or even a tall, cold bottle of diet coke. She politely thanked me and brought them into her room where she placed them carefully in her bedside drawer or closet. She did not need them or want them or even barely consider them for longer than it took to store them away.

Sometimes I think she was just getting ready for what was coming next. Her whole life she needed so little but where she was going, there was nothing she would need.

It's an aching, strange thing to go through your parents' belongings after they die. The day before mom's funeral, my brother and I began the process. There was nothing of great value but much that was precious, of course. One of the things I decided to take home with me was mom's jewelry box. It is pink with pink velveteen on the inside. As a child, I loved to open that pretty box and look at the treasures inside. When I opened it after her death, it still contained many of the same things she always had kept in there: some earrings she wore when she was right out of college and worked in Minneapolis, her high school Letter, a locket with a picture of dad, and dad's wedding ring. I took dad's ring and slipped it onto my thumb.

It was just a few days before that I put on mom's wedding ring. When she was in ICU, they had to take it off her since her fingers were swelling so badly. I put it into a plastic bag along with the only other piece of jewelry she wore, a Black Hills silver ring I had given her some years before. I told her I would hold onto them until she got out of the hospital. The night she died, while I was still in the hospital room trying to gather the strength to stand and go home, I kept looking at her hands and seeing the indent on her ring finger. I remembered the rings still in my purse. I took them out and slipped both those rings on my finger. I have not taken them off since then. I planned to bring them back to Minnesota and let them be buried with her, but when the time came, I realized I couldn't part with them. Her thin gold wedding band was on her hand her whole life. She held us as babies and took care of my father for decades while wearing that ring. It belonged with her, but I kept it. I needed it to help me get through the rest of my life without her.

It makes no sense that a thin gold band should help me feel closer to my beautiful mom who cared so little for material things. But maybe it does. It stood for a promise she made that mattered to her more than any other. I look at it, and I can see her hands still. Truthfully, I would give away every single material item I have before I would get rid of this ring. It rests on my finger right below my own wedding band. Like a reminder from my mom that promises and persistence matter. She's still teaching me, even now.

Once upon a time, the jewelry box clinked out a little tune. That was part of its' magic. Months after mom's death, after I brought the jewelry box with me to Texas and placed it on my dresser, I noticed the small key on the back. I turned the key to see if it still worked and there was only silence. I wish I remembered what song it used to play.

20-23 Good friend, follow your father's good advice; don't wander off from your mother's teachings. Wrap yourself in them from head to foot; wear them like a scarf around your neck. Wherever you walk, they'll guide you; whenever you rest, they'll guard you; when you wake up, they'll tell you what's next. For sound advice is a beacon, good teaching is a light, moral discipline is a life path. – Proverbs 6:20-23

Prayer: Dear God, I've learned so much from those who have gone before me. Thank you for all those who have guided me along the way so far. In Jesus' name, I pray. Amen.

Reflect: What material possessions do you have that are particularly meaningful to you? Why?

Viking Lutheran Church
Maddock, North Dakota

Things Happen

Last Summer, my older son had his tonsils taken out. We knew he wouldn't be feeling good after the surgery but had no idea the healing process was going to be as long or complex as it was. Our poor boy pretty much sat on the couch for a week, woke up during the night crying from the pain in his throat and ear, and lost thirteen pounds. After a week had gone by, it was time for both the boys to go to Bible camp in North Dakota but Owen was nowhere near ready to leave the couch yet. So, I left with our younger son, and Owen stayed home with my husband. We decided that if he was feeling better in a couple days, he would join us at camp.

Owen began to feel better, so he came to camp, but we found out that the loud noises of 100 other kids made his ear throb with pain. So, Owen spent much of his time with me in the Retreat Center. He watched movies and rested his ear on a heating pad. I read and wrote.

I take pictures of country churches. The smaller and more remote, the better, and being in North Dakota for a week I was excited to take some time prowling around the backroads and looking for churches. There was one I read about that I wanted to see but it was a couple of hours away. Owen decided to come with me on a day trip to find that church. We stopped at Walmart and found some little reusable warming pads to have on hand in case his ear started to bother him while we were out and away from electricity.

It was a splendid day. Somewhere in the middle of North Dakota, there was a crazy-good radio station that was playing some great stuff. The lyric, "may all your favorite bands stay together" caught my ear. The band was Dawes, and when the radio station faded out, I looked them up on Spotify and fell in love with them immediately.

Their songs became the soundtrack for that day as I was driving around the countryside of North Dakota with my eldest son, who is so nearly a teenager it takes my breath away. We rode along through sunshine and then pouring rain, along highways and then miles of gravel road until we found the little church we were looking for, Norway Lutheran in rural McHenry County.

Like a tale in a storybook, a man with a glass eye happened to be there, miles and miles from anywhere, in the middle of a prairie thunderstorm. He let us into the church and told us stories about that enchanting little place overflowing with history. We dodged the raindrops to run out the front door and around the corner of the church where he lifted the trap door to the cellar fellowship hall, and we went down to see the cute kitchen and gathering space and pore over old pictures.

Finally, Owen and I said our goodbyes with the nice man and headed back toward camp, talking about how cool that church had been. We laughed about how it was good that the man whom we had willingly followed into the cellar in the middle of nowhere had been very nice and not a psycho-killer. We stopped at some other churches on the way where I took photographs, and Owen did bottle flips on the front steps. We went to a truck-stop for supper. I had soup. He had 1/8 of a pancake (still not much appetite). The sun came out and the shadows were growing long.

Some people say they don't know where the time goes. Some people say they missed out on their kids growing up. But I know where the time goes. I have every second of it stored in my mind and heart. And I have not missed out on my kids growing. I have been here every day. I've reveled in their laughter, and I've dried their tears. I have shown them the joys of cupcakes, meteor showers, watching for the space station to fly over on a quiet Texas night, sledding for hours on a snowy Minnesota hill, watching a great movie, singing around a campfire. I've taught them to say, "thank you" and "I'm sorry" and "have a good day," to say their prayers, that love is the most important thing. I have understood how precious these days are. I have not taken a smidgen, an iota, the tiniest whit for granted.

Perhaps this is the one gift given to me in experiencing the deaths of my parents when my children were still very small: I know this day is the only one I get. Yesterday is over. Tomorrow is only a wish. Now is the time to love and to live.

> *"Lord, let me know my end,*
> *and what is the measure of my days;*
> *let me know how fleeting my life is.*
> *[5] You have made my days a few handbreadths,*
> *and my lifetime is as nothing in your sight.*
> *Surely everyone stands as a mere breath.*
> *[6] Surely everyone goes about like a shadow. – Psalm 39:4-6 (NRSV)*

Prayer: Dear God, help me stop, look around, notice all that I too often miss, and never stop giving you thanks. In Jesus' name, I pray. Amen.

Reflect: If today is unimaginably precious, and it is, what is one thing you want to be sure to do?

Norway Lutheran Church
McHenry County, North Dakota

<u>Finish Line</u>

My husband's parents died in 2007 – Butch in January and Dottie in August. Our eldest, Owen, was just one year old then and our baby, Jesse, was born in June of that year. The last time we saw Dottie was at Jesse's baptism just two weeks before she died.

It was a warm afternoon when my husband got a frantic call from his sister that their mother had died suddenly. We went down to New Mexico and Chad and his brothers and sister hobbled around the house in shock, making piles and going through papers while took care of the kiddos.

A few days later, I led the funeral service and wanted to do such a good job, but I didn't. I didn't know the perfect words to say for a loss like that. I know better what to say for strangers than for my own family. The same thing happened when my husband's dad was dying, and Dottie called to say he wanted to have communion one last time and asked if I could bring it to him. We were coming down to see them in a few days. I was happy if I could do something for him but I felt sick at the thought of how in the world to do this? How could I knit together words to pray a prayer out loud for my beloved's father in his last hours? I felt like I just barely knew how to be a daughter-in-law, I had no idea how to be a pastor to him, too. Butch was family, real family to me and I loved him. That was the problem. I knew I would weep sharing the sacrament with him. I knew I couldn't put on my 'pastor face' for him and be any sort of calm and comforting presence because I would just keep thinking about how sad I was for me and for Chad and for our boys and just everyone that we wouldn't have him around anymore. It would be too real, too close, too deep, too much. I called the hospice chaplain at the facility where he was hospitalized and asked her to bring him the sacrament. I told Dottie that I was worried we wouldn't get there in time. She said she understood.

Right before my own mother had her final heart surgery just weeks before her death, I spotted a hospital chaplain in the hallway and dragged him into her room in ICU. There was a good chance mom might not survive the surgery. I demanded he pray for her right then. I bowed my head while hot tears flowed down my face and onto her bedspread.

All the prayers I have said by hundreds of hospital beds, but I could not pray out loud for her. The silent prayers I lobbed toward heaven were incessant, but to speak those words aloud, if she were to hear them, I would have been undone. Not that I was very composed as it was, but I knew I was only capable of being her daughter, not her pastor.

There are times I cannot be the pastor because I need a pastor. There are times I need someone else to be saying the prayers and administering the sacraments. There are times I need to hear someone else speaking the holy and precious words of God to my grief, my joy, my life.

In seminary, I worked at a hospital in the Twin Cities, and a priest who worked there as well was recalling his mother's funeral. He said he had done the entire service himself. Back then I thought to myself how brave and wonderful it was to be able to do such a thing for his mother. However, now I see a different perspective. I feel sad that he couldn't just be a son grieving his mother. Was that how it was at every significant moment in his family's life together? Was he always expected to say the prayer, do the wedding, speak at the wake, give the last rites? Was he ever able just to be present as himself, not his role?

Sometimes I'm glad when my roles as pastor and as family member and friend intersect. I'll forever cherish presiding at my nephew's wedding and at the weddings of countless friends. I'm thrilled I could be the one to baptize my sons and I look forward to blessing them on their confirmation day.

However, I'm equally glad that at my parents' funerals I simply sat down and listened to the preacher speak. I let the congregation minister to me with their kind words and hugs. Once when I was preaching and tears sprang up as I told a hard story, a parishioner brought a tissue to me at the pulpit.

Thanks be to God for those who have ministered to their minister. There are so many of you.

In the same way, even though we are many individuals, Christ makes us one body and individuals who are connected to each other. – Romans 12:5

Be kind to one another, tender-hearted, forgiving each other, just as God in Christ also has forgiven you. – Ephesians 4:32

Prayer: Dear God, thank you for moments when I get to extend caring concern but also help me to remember to ask for help when I need it. In Jesus' name, I pray. Amen.

Reflect: Is it easy to ask for help when you need it? If not, what makes it hard to enlist the help of others? How do you feel when others ask you for help?

Lysne Lutheran Church
Hawley, Minnesota

Choose Life

There was a course I led some years ago based on a book called "Love and Logic" by Foster Cline and Jim Fay. The book and class were geared toward helping parents gain practical, effective, and fun techniques for fostering respect, responsibility, self-control, and good decision-making skills in children. One of the tools for getting your kiddos to listen to you was to give your kids control through giving them choices. The rules on the choices were that:

1. If the child doesn't choose, you had to be prepared to choose yourself.

2. You had to pick two choices you could live with.

3. Never give a choice unless you are willing to allow the child to live with the consequences of his/her bad choice.

An example of a good choice would be "Would you rather clean your room or rake the lawn so I'll have time to clean your room?

Or "Would you rather clean your room Saturday or Sunday?" or "Do you want to settle the problem yourselves or draw straws to see who sits by the window?"

So, it was one day that I found myself in a battle of wills with my eldest, Owen, who was only about three or four years old. We were standing in the kitchen, and I was trying to get him to pick up his toys. Being a toddler, he wasn't interested in what I was saying when suddenly I remembered the choices technique and I said, "Would you rather pick up your toys or – but I hadn't thought of the other choice before I started talking – so I said the first thing that came to mind, "Would you rather pick up your toys or I dump a cup of water on your head?"

I knew it maybe wasn't the best set of choices, but I recalled that follow-through was very important, so when he didn't pick up his toys, I walked over to the sink, filled a small cup with water and dumped it on his head.

It may not have been one of my finest parenting moments, and the Love and Logic people probably wouldn't like it because the choices aren't supposed to sound like threats, but it got his attention. He looked at me like he couldn't believe I did that and I said, "I told you, you had two choices." I gave him a towel to dry off his little head, and then he put his toys away.

God gives the people choices and reveals that a beautiful and prosperous way of living exists for those who choose God's way. *"Choose life,"* God says. (Deuteronomy 30:19)

Unfortunately, often when we think of God's commands we don't think of them in this life-giving way, but rather as a set of rules we better follow "or else." Do this and do that or the fires of hell await you. Do this and do that or God won't be happy. Even worse, God's laws often get translated into something like "if it is too fun, God probably frowns upon it."

I grew up in a home in which there was a long list of things that I was assured God didn't like: drinking, dancing, playing cards, spending time with people who weren't Lutheran, dating before the age of 18, long hair on boys, short hair on girls, tattoos, listening to loud music on Sundays, listening to rock music anytime, and spending money on anything frivolous. The God of my childhood was a stern taskmaster I couldn't please.

Perhaps that is why instead of veering way toward Law, I tend to veer way toward grace in my preaching and my work as a pastor. "Jesus loves you" is the message I want my kids and all kids to know the best. Forgiveness and mercy for mistakes made is the life-giving message the Christian church uniquely brings.

But the law has its place, an important place, and that is why Jesus' Sermon on the Mount (see Matthew 5) which began with the Beatitudes (blessed are the pure in heart, blessed are the poor in spirit) and continued with his instructions for being salt and light in the world, continues with laws. These laws aren't new to the people, but Jesus is expanding on them.

First, he talks about murder, *"You have heard it said, "you shall not murder"* but then he adds, *"But I say to you that if you are angry with a brother or sister, you will be liable to judgment and if you insult a brother or sister, you will be liable to the council."* He encourages that before making a gift to the altar of God, you are to make amends with anyone with whom you are fighting or have had harsh words."

Martin Luther expanded on this in his explanation of the ten commandments in the Small Catechism. Luther's meaning of the fifth commandment is: *We should fear and love God that we may not hurt nor harm our neighbor in his body, but help and befriend him in every bodily need.*

Anger is a normal, human emotion but we others and ourselves if we don't work hard to resolve anger. If it is anger about a wrong done to you, be patient with the feelings of anger, but do what you can to let go of those feelings. Don't forget, prayer helps with this process.

Sometimes we need to speak words of forgiveness, or sometimes we need to put as much distance as we can between ourselves and the person who has hurt us. C.S. Lewis, in his book *Mere Christianity*, wrote about the fact that loving one's neighbor does not mean liking them. *"Loving my enemies does not apparently mean thinking them nice either. That is an enormous relief. For a good many people think that forgiving your enemies means making out that they are really not such bad fellows after all, when it is quite plain that they are."* (*Mere Christianity, Book II Chapter 7*) This is where we can find the strength to forgive. Loving our enemies doesn't mean we think they are fantastic people or invite them out to coffee.

Righteous anger over injustice we see in the world can be a good thing - but not if it stays simple, crude anger. Only if that small hard stone of anger evolves into a seed for working for change can it do any good. Choose life, God says. Choose to let go of anger.

Next, Jesus talks about adultery, *"you have heard it said, 'you shall not commit adultery."* Jesus expands this so that we remember it's not just our actions that matter, but our thoughts. Don't entertain thoughts that might cause you to sin. Luther expanded on this in the Small Catechism saying: *"We should fear and love God that we may lead a chaste and decent life in words and deeds, and each love and honor his spouse."*

Jesus uses vivid imagery: *"If your right eye causes you to sin, tear it out and throw it away."* It's a powerful way of saying, "if you are attracted to your co-worker, don't start sharing personal things with each other. Don't confide in him or her in a way that starts feelings of intimacy to grow." We can't control whom we find attractive, but we can control our behavior. We must. The love shared between married partners is a gift from God, and as with any gift, it must be cherished and nurtured. This isn't always easy, but it is a holy and sacred task, nonetheless.

Choose life. Choose love. Choose faithfulness in your words and actions – But also this:

Sometimes relationships do break apart, and sometimes an end to the relationship is best if there is abuse or if trust gets so shattered it can't be repaired. Divorce happens, and when it does, remember grace. I know very few couples who have divorced without trying very hard to make things work. If divorce has been part of your journey, remember you are loved. Our vows and commitments we make to each other matter to God, but we matter even more. When things fall apart, God is still here to help us put the pieces back together and start again. Always.

God says to us, "Choose Life." Choosing life means paying attention to God's laws, taking them to heart, using them as our guidepost for living the best, most whole life possible. Choosing life also means we remember at the beginning, middle, and end of all our striving, there is grace.

[19] I call heaven and earth to witness against you today that I have set before you life and death, blessings and curses. Choose life so that you and your descendants may live, [20] loving the Lord your God, obeying him, and holding fast to him; for that means life to you and length of days, so that you may live in the land that the Lord swore to give to your ancestors, to Abraham, to Isaac, and to Jacob. – Deuteronomy 30:19-20

27-28 *"You know the next commandment pretty well, too: 'Don't go to bed with another's spouse.' But don't think you've preserved your virtue simply by staying out of bed. Your heart can be corrupted by lust even quicker than your body. Those leering looks you think nobody notices—they also corrupt.*

29-30 *"Let's not pretend this is easier than it really is. If you want to live a morally pure life, here's what you have to do: You have to blind your right eye the moment you catch it in a lustful leer. You have to choose to live one-eyed or else be dumped on a moral trash pile. And you have to chop off your right hand the moment you notice it raised threateningly. Better a bloody stump than your entire being discarded for good in the dump. –* *Matthew 5:27-30*

Prayer: Dear God, help me to be faithful to all the promises I have made and listen attentively for the guidance of the Holy Spirit in every situation. In Jesus' name, I pray. Amen.

Reflect: Am I satisfied with the choices I have made? Are there any I would change if I could? How might I make better choices moving forward?

Upsala Lutheran Church
Calloway, Minnesota

Extraordinary

In the church basement, we are collecting items for the next rummage sale. There are tons of decorations, bookshelves, lamps, clothes and dishware, odds and ends of every sort, including books. This week someone dropped off two huge bags filled only with dieting books. There was "Wheat Belly," the "17-Day Diet," old guides from Jenny Craig and Weight Watchers Points booklets; it was a small weight loss library.

As I looked through the books, I wondered how many broken dreams were between those pages. How many times had this person bought a new diet book and thought, "This time! This time it will work. This diet will be the one." Maybe some of those diets did "work" for a while, but apparently not forever, because more diet books were purchased. I thought about all the wasted time and money in those two huge bags of books. What great things could this person have accomplished in the hours that were spent counting calories and grams of some flavorless low-fat concoction? How might this person's life had been more productive if instead of recording the number of minutes of cardio at the gym, he or she had learned a new hobby or written a letter, a book, a poem? What made this person decide to get rid of these books finally?

Mostly I thought about how I did the same thing a few years ago. I gave away at least a couple big bags full of dieting books to Goodwill. It became clear to me that life was too short for one more minute of the craziness of worrying about how much I weigh. With all the delicious food in the world, I couldn't bear only to eat oatmeal or egg whites for breakfast anymore. Determining how good or bad my day was by whether or not I stuck to a specific plan or an allotted amount of calories had done nothing to benefit my life. I finally realized it was madness to give so much time and energy and money toward trying so hard to be 'less' in any way. I said a giant "NO" to the diet industry and sighed a relieved "YES!" to life and listening to myself, my body and my wishes and wants.

However, it's hard to learn to listen to your body after spending decades trying to bend your body into submission. From the age of 12 until decades later, I knew I was too big, too hungry, too much in every way and the only solution was to battle myself until I reached that elusive smaller size. I learned how to be good at starving. I mastered self-control, and to say, "I'll have a Diet Coke" when everyone around me had ice cream. Occasionally I did shrink almost as small as I wanted to be but it was never enough and impossible to sustain. I was hungry, weighing myself constantly, irritable, until finally, I had to eat. Usually everything in sight. That is what happens after you starve, you binge.

Dieting is always about restriction, and restriction almost always produces binging. It's a tiny percentage of people who lose weight and can keep it off, and those who regain weight often end up heavier than they were before they started trying to lose weight. In fact, I heard one researcher put it this way: the most effective way to gain weight in the long run is to go on a diet. It's madness.

I'm finally listening to my body and my cravings – for food and movement. I choose to eat spinach and drink water because I like how they make me feel. I choose to enjoy a piece of cake with my kids because cake (especially frosting!) is a beautiful thing. I run most mornings because it makes me happy. I no longer hate anything about the space I take up in the world, and I thank God for this strong, healthy body.

I pray that whoever dropped off those bags of books in the church basement has found peace and joy in her or his skin, too. I pray they move their bodies for the love of it and eat exactly what they want to eat today.

"I praise you because I am fearfully and wonderfully made; your works are wonderful, I know that full well." – Psalm 139:14

Prayer: Dear God, thank you for nutritious, sustaining, and delicious food to eat. Thank you for my body. Help me to treat it well. In Jesus' name, I pray. Amen.

Reflect: Are you ever hard on yourself for the way you look? Right now, list five things you appreciate about the body God gave you. What is something you can do today to take good, nurturing care of yourself?

Tunbridge Lutheran Church
Pierce County, North Dakota

White Supremacy is Sin. Say it.

I have visited Norway a few times. My great-grandparents who left Norway were people I never met, but I wanted to see and explore the homeland they left behind. While I may know next to nothing about my great-grandparents, Johanna and Halvor Haugen and Jonas and Ane Hetland, I've seen places they walked, felt the sunlight on my skin there, touched the baptismal font where my great-grandfather was baptized. These people are strangers to me and yet they are part of me.

In the summertime, Norway is full of people researching their ancestry and visiting ancestral family farms and villages. There is something deeply meaningful about standing where your ancestors stood. Just as a tree dies if it is cut off from its roots, something inside us dies if we lose touch with the places from which we come.

Our roots matter. That's why people gather for family reunions to stay connected with the cousins and generations and pass down stories and family trees. That's why churches mark significant anniversaries and take time to recount the events that have happened over the decades. It's why New Year's Eve always has a little bit of a haunting feeling to it. We think back over all that the last year held and the years before it, too. Where have we been? Where are we going? What is being written on the pages of the stories of our lives? How can we make the next chapter the best it can be?

Our roots as Christian people matter. If it weren't so, we wouldn't spend time every Sunday recounting the stories from the Bible. We find our history as God's people and our direction for how to live by studying God's word.

And our roots as a nation matter. We remember not just the good stuff so we can pat ourselves on the back, but we remember the bad stuff because it can help us make better choices now. Hopefully. You would think this would be, true, but human beings seem to have short memories.

That's the only explanation I can think of for why white supremacists and neo-Nazi gatherings still exist. The headlines in the summer of 2017 told of how in Charlottesville, Virginia, a group of White Nationalists chanting, "White Lives Matter" and "We Will Not Be Replaced" met at the same time as there was another group there celebrating peace and diversity. Some of our ELCA brothers and sisters were there with a group advocating for peace and diversity. They gathered in a church, singing and praying, while the white nationalists surrounded the church, yelling, bearing torches and refused to let those in the church come out. Those who were there say it was terrifying and like nothing they had ever experienced before. This was just the beginning of the horror as in the days that followed there was bloodshed, injury and even the death of one of the peaceful protestors, Heather Heyer, by a white, racist terrorist driving a vehicle through a crowd.

My first thought when I heard about it was that it was far away from my little church in northwestern Minnesota. But the next day there was an interview with a white supremacist in Fargo, North Dakota, a city only 45 minutes away. It is becoming clear that while this is one of those things that feels like an earthquake far away, the tremors of it are much closer to all of us than we think.

I confess I have been guilty of thinking that racism isn't actually 'a thing' anymore. I remember saying that not so long ago. I said it because I have friends of all races, and segregation and all that was a long time ago, and we are all supposed to be equal, right? So why are we even still talking about this?

But then I learned that point of view is a luxury of people who enjoy privilege. People who are marginalized don't ever get that luxury.

I received my Doctor of Ministry degree at a diverse seminary in Denver, Iliff School of Theology. In my class, many different faiths and races were represented. The summer seminar was on racism, and I was deep in my thinking that this was all kind of "ho-hum", that racism wasn't a thing anymore.

One of the professors led an exercise with our class I will never forget. She asked us to each tell what our first impression of other members of the class would be if we only saw each other on the street or had just briefly met each other.

I thought it was ridiculous and a waste of time. I glanced at my watch as the first person who tried this practice, Veronica, a black woman, offered to give her first impression of me. She said she assumed I was wealthy and had always been wealthy, that I probably lived in a nice suburban house, that I liked to shop, that the church I served was all white and in a nice part of town.

I forget everything she said, but I remember feeling a little like I had been punched. Even though I knew this was just an exercise for a class, I was angry that she judged me based on the color of my skin and what she thought she knew of me. I was ticked off she assumed I was rich and I had never wanted for anything. How dare she think my journey had been one of ease and security when the truth was that my childhood had known its' share of food stamps and government cheese and wearing the same pair of jeans and shoes every day because that is all I had for school. How dare she think that she really knew me...

And then I got it. I realized the exercise our professor was trying to do with us had worked perfectly because, for the first time, I understood the smallest speck of what it felt like to experience racism. I experienced the teensiest iota of what it feels like to be subject to someone thinking they had me all figured out just because of the color of my skin.

That exercise informed me of my privilege. Most of us don't feel like we are super privileged, and yet we have more privilege than we realize. I am a good example. As a middle-aged white woman, I could go walking anywhere, linger in an aisle of any store, sit on a park bench for any length of time, and go relatively unnoticed. Few people would stop to question if I am up to something. This would not be the case if I were a black teenager. It's unfair but it is true, and this kind of thing is called privilege. It is an advantage someone carries around not because they earned it but because they were born into it.

With privilege comes responsibility and being followers of Jesus comes responsibility: to stand up for those who do not share in that privilege. Jesus always was on the side of those who were marginalized and so we must be as well.

White supremacist gatherings are a cancer, an infection. They need to be called out and cut out, recognized and eradicated as quickly as possible or they can slowly poison the rest of the body.

The stock I come from, Lutherans with Scandinavian roots, have a history of wanting to be nice and not wanting to make waves – but we must learn to be brave to say, "that is not okay" when we hear the racist joke or remark because otherwise, we contribute to the cancer of racism. It's like Martin Luther King, Jr. said, "In the end we will not remember the words of our enemies but the silence of our friends." Dear God, help us not to be silent when faced with racism.

It was chilling to see on the news reports that several of the white nationalist young men were wearing crosses around their necks as they shouted words of hate. They wore crosses. Shame on us if we don't teach our children better than that. To be a Christian is the opposite of hate like that. To be a follower of Jesus Christ is to speak love and peace and hope to all God's children. Dear God, help us to raise up our children in the church better than that.

And while we need to be vocal to shut down voices of hate, we need to learn to be quiet and listen when those who are oppressed are trying to speak. Everyone needs to be heard. We all need to know our stories matter to one another and to God.

There's a great example of this in scripture. A Canaanite woman approaches Jesus. She needs help for her daughter, yet she just doesn't count as a real person. Nor does her daughter. Jesus' disciples want Jesus to send her away, and Jesus seems to agree. Jesus refuses to meet her, dismissing her because she is not an Israelite, he says: *"I was sent only to the lost sheep of Israel"*. She kneels before Jesus, and he calls her a dog. Jesus and his disciples deny this woman's humanity. It's a difficult story. It doesn't paint Jesus in a pretty light.

The Canaanite woman struggles to be heard. She cries out. She kneels, begs. Jesus rejects her. Finally, she says something so clever that Jesus grants her request. She is the only person who wins an argument with Jesus.

So many are still crying out to be heard. Church, let's work harder to be good at listening.

In the twisted, tangled roots of our nation, there is a history of strife between races. Horrible injustices have happened, most at the hands of white people. There has also been healing, a healing that is slow and was fought for by so many. Now we get to guard the healing that has begun so that it continues. We have a holy and urgent task to make certain our children and grandchildren grow up knowing that every person regardless of race, religion, social status, ethnicity, gender or sexual orientation has unsurpassed worth in the eyes of God. We say it out loud again and again so that there is no mistaking who we are: followers of Jesus Christ, a brown-skinned, middle-eastern Jew, who taught us unequivocally that God's love is for all and that white supremacy is sin.

[25] But she came and knelt before him, saying, "Lord, help me." [26] He answered, "It is not fair to take the children's food and throw it to the dogs." [27] She said, "Yes, Lord, yet even the dogs eat the crumbs that fall from their masters' table." [28] Then Jesus answered her, "Woman, great is your faith! Let it be done for you as you wish." And her daughter was healed instantly. – Matthew 15:25-28

[28-29] In Christ's family there can be no division into Jew and non-Jew, slave and free, male and female. Among us you are all equal. That is, we are all in a common relationship with Jesus Christ. – Galatians 3:28

Prayer: Dear God, you created us all to be equal. Help me to remember I am no better and no worse than anyone else. In Jesus' name, I pray. Amen.

Reflect: Do you think racism is still a "thing"? What are ways we can become more in tune with struggles of others?

Heskestad Church
Rogaland County, Norway

When You Can't Get Along

For the better part of two years, she didn't speak to me. When I saw her at church or downtown, she pretended not to see me. She skipped the line to shake my hand after worship.

I suppose I'm normal in that I hate conflict. I loathe it with the fire of a thousand suns. Yet, I knew I needed to do something. I tried to reach out to her by brightly saying "hello" when I saw her; then, by calling and leaving her messages to call me back. She responded with more silence for months and months until one day the phone rang and it was her.

"You ignored me," she said. I asked her when I ignored her and she said that one day, shortly after I arrived at that church, I walked up to a group of people where she was standing and "you said 'hello' to everyone in that circle of people except me."

I remembered the day. It was a beautiful, warm fall day. I saw the group standing outside as I was on my way to the church from the parsonage. A friend of mine from home was visiting, and I wanted to introduce him to the group so as we walked over I was going over everyone's names in my head. I remember being proud of myself because I could remember each name. When we got to the group, I introduced him to each person by name, or so I thought. In my nervousness I forgot her, or maybe because I had been practicing all the names in my head, I thought I said her name already, but I hadn't. However it happened, she felt snubbed, and she had never forgotten it.

I did the only thing there was to do, I apologized to her. I admitted I could be so scatter-brained sometimes and I asked her to please forgive me. I was sorry I had hurt her, so deeply sorry. (Even though, to tell you the truth, inside I was feeling hurt and angry for getting the silent treatment for so very long.) But I said, "I'm sorry." And She said, "I forgive you."

Saint Matthew writes in his gospel (Matt. 18:15-17) about how we as Christian people are to deal with conflict. In fact, in many church constitutions and the constitution of the entire Evangelical Lutheran Church in America, this is our method for dealing with any conflict in the church. First, you talk face to face. Then, if it isn't worked out, you talk about it in the presence of one or two others, and try again. Then, finally, in the presence of the church. Now keep in mind that "the church" here was often groups of people who met in homes, so it wasn't like bringing it up at a huge congregational meeting, it was like discussing it with a living room full of people.

What's interesting is that in the New Revised Standard Version, verse 17 reads, *"If the member refuses to listen to them, tell it to the church; and if the offender refuses to listen even to the church, let such a one be to you as a Gentile and a tax collector."* We might think the scripture is saying it's time to cast that person out, put them outside the community, but then we recall how Jesus treated the outsiders, the tax collectors, that Saint Matthew himself was a tax collector. Jesus was always trying to draw everyone into community.

Matthew isn't proposing that we cast the person out, he's encouraging us to double down on our efforts. That's why I like how Eugene Peterson's, "The Message" puts verse 17, *"If he won't listen to the church, you'll have to start over from scratch, confront him with the need for repentance, and offer again God's forgiving love."*

This scripture is not a quick and easy recipe for conflict resolution but an unending process. It's like when Jesus is asked how many times we are expected to forgive and he says seventy times seven. (Matt. 18:22) He wasn't telling them to do some mental math and then forgive others exactly 490 times. Rather, those numbers signified an infinite amount – forgive infinitely. And in turn, when we look to heal hurting relationships we keep trying.

This is never to say that an abusive relationship should be allowed to continue. There has to be mutual love, mutual forgiveness, mutual humility, mutual grace. Sometimes that never comes, and then we entrust that person to God and move on.

But sometimes reconciliation happens in the most surprising ways. Even when we never thought it could. By God's grace.

Do you have a relationship you think can never heal? Has so much time and hurt happened that it is impossible for things to mend? Maybe you have no idea what to do anymore. Don't give up.

Because you never know what God can do.

And because there is always something you can do.

My apology to the woman from my church was either too little or too late because our relationship didn't improve. We had said the I'm sorry's and the I forgive you's – but something was damaged permanently. Maybe I continued to be scatter-brained and forgot something else. Maybe she just realized she wanted a different pastor. Even though we both made small attempts to reach out to each other, over time she drifted away and began to worship elsewhere. I moved away and nearly fifteen years have passed since I last saw her.

But I still think about her. I think about how she clung to her hurt, and I did, too. I think about what I might have said or done differently. I may never see her again in this life and I may not ever understand why we were like oil and water, but I do one thing I am able to do: I pray for her. Still. All these years later. I pray for her joy, for her family, that her life is good and peaceful. And that brings healing of its' own for me. I trust and hope in God's provision that somehow it might bring healing for her as well.

There is something we can do when relationships seem broken beyond fixing. We can pray. And it is quite something the peace that can bring.

God doesn't call us to be best of friends with everyone. God made us too unique for that to be possible all the time. But God did create us to seek peace, to work toward understanding, to, as Paul says in Romans, *"love other people as well as you do yourself."*

Let's do that with our words.

Let's do that with our actions.

Let's do that with our prayers.

15-17 "If a fellow believer hurts you, go and tell him—work it out between the two of you. If he listens, you've made a friend. If he won't listen, take one or two others along so that the presence of witnesses will keep things honest, and try again. If he still won't listen, tell the church. If he won't listen to the church, you'll have to start over from scratch, confront him with the need for repentance, and offer again God's forgiving love. – Matthew 18:15-17 (The Message MSG)

Be joyful in hope, patient in affliction, faithful in prayer. – Romans 12:12

Prayer: Dear God, help me to be loving toward the people you have put in my life, and when that feels impossible, never let me stop praying for them. Not necessarily because they need to be changed through my prayers, but because I do. In Jesus' name, I pray. Amen.

Reflect: Who do you need to forgive? Who are you hoping will someday forgive you? Is there some way you can still reach out to that person and work to heal that relationship? Even if you have tried before, are you willing try again?

Cemetery statue at Bakke Lutheran Church
Detroit Lakes, Minnesota

<u>So it Goes</u>

I am afraid of the grief leaving me.

The weather is starting to cool off a little bit here in Texas. Funny that it being in the eighties is 'cooling off,' but that's how it is here. September is nearing an end.

It was the season of autumn when mom and I were dancing together from the nursing home to the cardiologist to different hospital stays. It was like a terrible jig in which the steps got harder, and the music got terribly unpleasant and we tried to stay together until ultimately, we collapsed in a heap of silence and stillness.

I miss her so deeply and fully. It's the most significant feeling I can feel anymore – this grief and this emptiness. I can feel other things, surely – pride in my children and joy in the things they do. I feel love for them and Chad. I feel peace in my work and my church, and I can feel annoyed when people disagree with me or if things don't move at a pace I enjoy. But the only feeling that has defined me since I lost her is this grief.

But sometimes now, and this is the scary thing: I feel like I might survive it. And if I survive it, then I will come out on the other side somehow. I feel like the strands of this darkness are getting more slippery and I know God is healing me, but I am terrified of it.

"Don't leave me breathing,
no, not alone,
There's so much more I meant to tell you.
I went by with flowers just to see,
But the granite told me you're still gone."
(from the song, "So It Goes" by Chris Pureka)

As long as I keep carrying this sadness, I'll know it was true that I loved her.

The part of me that died when she died is dear to me. I don't want it to live again. I want that empty space to remain as a monument to her. I don't want it to be filled. The ache of it reminds me of all I have lost – all that I had when I had a mom so beautiful.

God is our refuge and strength, an ever-present help in trouble. Therefore, we will not fear, though the earth give way and the mountains fall into the heart of the sea. – Psalm 46:1-2

Prayer: Dear God, grief is complicated and has shifted my world entirely. Be near to me and give me strength to face this ongoing storm. In Jesus' name, I pray. Amen.

Reflect: C.S. Lewis wrote, *"No one ever told me that grief felt so like fear."* What do you think of this statement? How do you find grief and fear to be similar?

Jostedal Church
Sogn og Fjordane, Norway

What Brings You Life?

In the fall of 1988, I was a freshman in college. I lived in a dorm on campus and it was there I made some of my best friends to this day. The rooms were so small that we spilled out into the hallways and found our own little community there – talking, ordering pizza, listening to the Indigo Girls, 10,000 Maniacs, and John Denver, and figuring out life together day by day.

Some people have wild and crazy college memories, but my friends and I enjoyed quieter pursuits: camping, biking, a lot of cookie-baking. One night my friend Mary and I wanted to make cookies, and so we went down to the tiny kitchen of the dorm. We had most of the ingredients on hand, except for sugar. It was a blizzard outside, and since we didn't want to venture to the store, we decided to go to the neighbor's house to borrow a cup of sugar. That house belonged to our college president. We walked over, rang the doorbell, and like good neighbors he and his wife gave us a cup of sugar. On the way back, Mary was carrying the cup of sugar and she slipped on an icy patch, the sugar flying into the air and swirling with the snow. So, we picked up the measuring cup and went back to President Dovre's house and asked for one more cup of sugar.

We laughed so hard that night. It seemed at every turn during college we found ridiculously fun, carefree, hilarious moments.

But there were difficult times, too. I was always writing in my journal and I wish I could sit down with the girl who wrote all those pages. I would invite her to breathe, invite her to lean into the things and people that bring her joy and life, rather than work so hard to fit in. I'd tell to cut out the dieting and stop obsessing about finding true love. I'd tell her, "Love finds you when the time is right and there is no stopping it. In the meantime, enjoy your friends, talk, listen to music, adventure, be."

Of course, it is easy to see life more clearly with the advantage of a few more decades lived. The truth is that there's so much we can't know until we live into it.

Recently, I preached at an evening worship service at my alma mater, and they told me the theme for this year's Campus Ministry is "Seeking." College is such a seeking time, but so is the rest of life. Every single stage, we are merely viewing life from different vantage points. Finding our way. Living into it.

We are always asking ourselves big questions: Should I venture down this path or that one? Should I take the new job or stay in my old one a little longer? What does God want me to do? How do I know where God is leading me? We are finding out what suits us and what doesn't. What brings us joy and what doesn't. What brings us life and what doesn't – that is a big one. Do you ask yourself, "what brings me life?"

This questioning, seeking, and searching is a holy task. Jesus repeatedly talks about seeking, finding answers through prayer, the guidance and presence of the Holy Spirit, the Spirit of Life. He knew we would feel lost sometimes, that we wouldn't always know the direction to go, the choice to make, and assured us that we aren't alone. God's Spirit is with us and in us, guiding us, yet often we need help listening for the guidance of that Spirit.

Want some help hearing the whisper of the Holy Spirit? Here's a clue: *pay close attention to what gives you life.*

When you notice worry, anger, fear, or anxiety, that can give you clues as to what the Spirit of God is leading you away from. In contrast, when you notice feelings of peace, patience, kindness, or any of the fruit of the Spirit, you are noticing what the Spirit of God is leading you toward.

Those things and people and places that bring you life and joy – lean into those. Where we sense any of the fruit of the Spirit – love, joy, peace, patience, kindness, goodness, faithfulness, gentleness, and self-control – the Holy Spirit works through those things to tell us more about who God is and what we are being called toward. As Paul writes, *"for God did not give us a spirit of cowardice, but rather a spirit of power and of love and of self-discipline*." The Holy Spirit is in motion. God loves us just as we are, but way too much to leave us perpetually the same.

When I returned to my college to preach at that evening service, it was the first time I had been in the that chapel for many, many years. It's funny, isn't it, how when you walk into a place where you haven't been for a long time, you expect it to look just like it did before? I had pictured it all in my mind how it was going to be, a full chapel, the hushed lights of the evening service, I'd be up on the podium in the spotlight just like the esteemed campus pastors when I was a student there.

But it turns out those evening communion services are not the same as they used to be anymore. There were about fifty there, and they said that was good attendance these days. There was no podium, no spotlight, not even a microphone. I found myself feeling strange and dismayed. This was not the way I remembered it!

But as the evening went on, my spirits lifted. The service was joyful and those gathered stayed for fellowship afterward. We sang gorgeous worship songs and new liturgies I had never heard before - and I remembered different can be very good. Indeed, different can be holy.

Everywhere, at every season of life, we need to listen for the motion of the Spirit because it is never calling us to stay the same. We don't have to fear changes. We can embrace the changes, trusting God is guiding us as we notice where the Spirit is bearing fruit both around us and in us.

What are you good at doing?

What do you enjoy doing so much that when you are doing it, you lose track of time?

What moves you, stirs you, brings you joy, inexplicably beckons you to something greater than yourself?

Listen to these questions and their answers. Listen to your life and trust this is holy work. The Spirit is still speaking, whispering to you of all that is yet possible, all that you might still become.

[22] But the fruit of the Spirit is love, joy, peace, forbearance, kindness, goodness, faithfulness, [23] gentleness and self-control. Against such things there is no law. - Galatians 5:22 (NIV)

Prayer: Dear God, help me to listen for Your wisdom and inspiration. Help me pay attention. Help me listen to this one life you have given me. In Jesus' name, I pray. Amen.

Reflect: What brings you life? What energizes and excites you? How can you include more of that in your day today?

The abandoned Immanuel Lutheran Church
Maddock, North Dakota

Holding up the Sky

It was a cool October morning when the doctor sat down with my infant son and me in the hospital waiting room. My mother was gravely ill. He fumbled with his pen as he explained that she was "a very, very sick lady" and that she probably would not survive.

He left the room, and I held the baby close. I could hear the sounds of people in the hallways, the sounds of the elevator doors opening and closing around the corner. How could people be going about life as usual when the entire world had obviously just shifted? My mother was dying.

My cell phone rang then and it was my friend, Amy. I told her where I was and what was happening. Within two hours she was sitting next to me, which means she had packed up her baby daughter and started heading up the freeway immediately. She didn't ask if she should come. She just came.

We didn't talk much during the hours she was there. There wasn't much to say. We just sat and held the babies, drank coffee, and fielded updates from the doctors and nurses. Her presence in that waiting room helped hold the sky in place when it felt like everything was about to come crashing down.

And above all these put on love, which binds everything together in perfect harmony. – Colossians 3:14

Prayer: Dear God, thank you for my friends. Help me be a good friend. In Jesus' name, I pray. Amen.

Reflect: Who has helped "hold up the sky" for you?

Grong Lutheran Church
Rollag, Minnesota

Burned

Twenty-one years ago, on Halloween, I left an internship at a church in Wyoming. I was supposed to be there for a whole year but ended up being there two months. Daily verbal abuse from my internship supervisor and crushing loneliness eventually took their toll until finally I packed up my car and cats and left.

I didn't think I would return to seminary or the path leading me to ordained ministry. I believed I was out for good, done like dinner, unfit to serve God as a pastor. I didn't know what I was going to do, but it was apparently going to be something else. Bridge burned. Over. I didn't say goodbye to a soul. I didn't even go back to my office to pick up my books, I just started driving east and vowed to never return to that sorry town.

But then, a few months later, after a whole lot of beer and prayer, I did go back to seminary and went on to complete another internship, and now I have been a pastor for 18 years and a few months.

Recently, I had lunch with a friend who is in seminary and just found out she is leaving her extremely unhealthy internship church. Unlike me, she is going about her ending differently and better: she told the bishop about all that she was going through, she got help, and the bishop is getting her out of there and into a different, hopefully healthier church. She asked for help, and she got it.

I wish I had known how to demand help twenty-one years ago. Instead, I drowned in the shame that I hated where I was, and I hated how my supervisor was speaking to me. I blamed myself. I fully believed that if I were just better/stronger/more outgoing/prettier/thinner/etc., my supervisor would be nice to me and I wouldn't feel like I was going to die every time I drove up to that church. I did talk to my seminary about how bad things were, but their efforts to help were minimal and came far too late. I wish I had demanded they listen to me. I wish I would have cried out louder for someone to hear me and help me. Instead, I tried for two months to suck it up and tough it out until I realized the survival of something deep within me was at stake.

It was dawn when I drove away. I smoked ten thousand cigarettes and cried an ocean. I said, "I'm sorry, God" on repeat until I crossed the Wyoming/South Dakota border. I was overcome with sadness and defeat. Even when I finally did go back to seminary, I slunk around the halls trying to take up as little space as possible. I felt called to be there, but I wished I could be invisible. I didn't want to talk about what had happened. I avoided people, barely making eye contact. It was only when I began to talk about what happened that I began to heal.

It's so long ago now, and I hardly ever think of it except for when I talk with someone else who is having a hard time maneuvering through some hurdle of life. I listen to how they are handling it, and I think about that harsh autumn in Wyoming.

I hadn't known how to demand help. That is not surprising. I was raised not to make a fuss, to deal with problems quietly, secretly even. It's like Dar Williams sings in her song, "Iowa:"

> "But way back where I come from,
> We never mean to bother,
> We don't like to make our passions other people's concern,
> And we walk in the world of safe people,
> And at night we walk into our houses and burn."

Growing up, I never knew anyone who spoke about their negative feelings. I watched people bottle up emotions until they exploded in anger, tears, or were submerged in alcohol. Problems weren't tackled as challenges, they were seen as a sign of failure and a source of shame. The only solution was silence and secrecy.

The last twenty-one years have been a long process of learning as an adult how to communicate and express all the feelings – including the unpleasant ones. I still have plenty of room to grow when it comes to communication, but I am good at defending my right to do what I feel called toward and staying away from what steals my joy. I don't have the patience for toxic people or toxic situations anymore. I don't feel I must suffer them. Somehow making up my mind about that must have changed something in the air around me, because while I used to seem to attract toxicity, I no longer do.

I think about how I would have handled my Wyoming internship if I encountered it later in life than I did. It is impossible to know. However, by now I do know that at some point each one of us must face an awful or even evil person, a horrible situation, get monumentally ticked off, and then see what we do. I could look back that time and see it as I did for a very long time: weakness because I didn't leave gracefully, because I didn't know how to respond perfectly...OR...I can see it as I choose to see it now: strength – how I took a baseball bat to that experience and smashed it when I realized it was killing me. My departure may not have been smooth, but it was effective.

And while the experience was devastating, as is often the case, beauty came out of the ashes of it: dear friends, adventures, travel, even getting reacquainted with the man I eventually married – so much good came out of leaving that awful internship. In the long run, it didn't matter how I left, all that matters was that I did. For all the pain that short period of time brought, no one would hardly remember it anymore except that I still feel the need to tell the story now and then.

Telling our hard stories can be medicinal, life-saving. I would never have believed it when I was growing up and so busy learning how to keep secrets and isolate when there was any kind of trouble. When we have a survival story to tell, it cuts us when we keep it inside, but it heals us when we tell it. Our survival stories assure others that they will survive, too. Telling the truth and sharing compassion is so much better than hiding in the safety of silence.

So, twenty-one years ago on Halloween night, I was at a Bible Camp in North Dakota. I drove directly there after I left Wyoming because the director was a friend of mine. I had an immense, all-consuming crush on him. Perhaps I was hoping my terrible, horrible, no-good, very bad luck would start turning around and he would turn into Prince Charming and sweep me away from the craptastic pile of manure my life felt like that night. That didn't happen. But, he did build me a fire and let me sleep on a couch in the retreat center. He didn't ask any questions about why I was roaming like a cigarette-smoke covered ghost through North Dakota on a cold October night; he just gave me a "hello friend" hug and a warm place to stay. I stared at the fire until I fell asleep, and left before dawn to keep driving. I made it the rest of the way to my parents' house in Minnesota and mom welcomed me in. She had my favorite supper waiting.

3-5 There's more to come: We continue to shout our praise even when we're hemmed in with troubles, because we know how troubles can develop passionate patience in us, and how that patience in turn forges the tempered steel of virtue, keeping us alert for whatever God will do next. In alert expectancy such as this, we're never left feeling shortchanged. Quite the contrary—we can't round up enough containers to hold everything God generously pours into our lives through the Holy Spirit! - Romans 5:3-5 The Message (MSG)

Prayer: Dear God, sometimes my troubles seem too heavy to carry. Bring me your peace that passes all understanding. In Jesus' name, I pray. Amen.

Reflect: Are there bridges you have burned in your life? Why? Is there anything you would do differently now as you look back?

Saint Peter's Lutheran and an impending summer storm
Becker County, Minnesota

Where is Lutheran? (A Message for Reformation Sunday)

The presiding bishop of the Evangelical Lutheran Church in America, Elizabeth Eaton, wrote a humorous story in the Lutheran magazine, *"A first-call candidate came to me about an interesting encounter she had with a waitress. The waitress admired our candidate's Luther Rose pendant and asked what it was. 'It's Lutheran,' replied the candidate. 'Where's Lutheran?' asked the waitress."*

She said they chuckled that the waitress imagined a place of beauty and mystery called Lutheran and they were also a little rueful that she had never heard the word 'Lutheran' before.

Growing up where I did in rural Minnesota, Lutherans were in the majority. In my little town of 700 people, there were three Lutheran churches in town plus three more in different directions out in the country. It was a change for me when I moved to other parts of the country where people didn't automatically know what a Lutheran was, were shocked to see a female pastor, or failed to recognize what my clergy collar signified.

Before I was married, when I was on an internship in Wyoming, there was a Sunday I was invited out to lunch with a family after church. I was wearing my clergy collar, and as we were escorted to our seats we passed a table with a couple of handsome, smart-looking fellows who looked to be around my age. I gave them a little smile as I passed by, as one does, and I heard one of the guys say to the other one, "did you see her? That nun was flirting with you."

I didn't go back and explain to him that I was not a nun, but I did begin to realize that the language of Lutheranism I had been speaking my whole life was not a language everyone spoke. It seems that even within the Lutheran church we can all get a little confused about our fundamental beliefs and what sets us apart from other denominations when we hear so many other theologies from various sources all the time.

So, what does set us apart as Lutherans?

I'll tell you right now what is remarkable about being Lutheran. It has nothing to do with us or Martin Luther, but it has everything to do with God. It is God's ridiculous, extravagant notion of grace.

There was a story I heard that illustrated grace perfectly: A woman was shopping when a man attempted to steal her wallet from her purse. She stopped him, but instead of notifying the authorities, she told him that if he came with her to the checkout, she would pay for his groceries. And that is exactly what she did.

Was that what the man deserved? Most likely we would say he deserved punishment for trying to take what wasn't his, but instead of calling the police, the woman decided to bless him and give him a gift.

That is grace right there.

And God's grace is receiving God's love and forgiveness - but not because we deserve it. Do good, give generously, forgive others, but it isn't any of those things that earn salvation for us. We can do nothing to earn God's love. It is a complete gift.

We need God's presence in our lives to bring about any good or blessing from us. That's why we confess every week, *"we are by nature sinful and unclean, and that we have sinned against Thee by thought, word and deed."* We are confessing that we are as Luther said, *"in bondage to sin and cannot free ourselves."* Lutherans believe that all that could ever be done to achieve our salvation was done on the cross by Jesus.

That is why for the Lutheran, the language we hear much of the time throughout the Christian church about accepting Jesus and deciding to follow Jesus should strike us as not quite right. Lutheran theology focuses on God's activity, not ours.

For example, while someone from another Christian denomination might say something like "I accepted Jesus into my heart" the Lutheran would say, "Jesus came into my heart". While others might say, "I have decided to live like a believer," the Lutheran would say, "Jesus love compels me to follow him." Others might say, "I was saved when I answered an altar call when I was twelve years old." Lutherans would say, "Jesus saved me when he died on the cross." Do you see the difference? Others may emphasize what human beings can do to get to God, but for Lutherans, it's all about what God has done and still does to get to us or perhaps more appropriately, stay with us.

Even being able to say, "I Believe" is a gift. Martin Luther wrote in the Small Catechism, *"I believe that I cannot by my own reason or strength believe in Jesus Christ, my Lord, or come to Him; but the Holy Spirit has called me by the Gospel, enlightened me with His gifts, sanctified and kept me in the true faith."*

That is why we encourage that babies be baptized and that one doesn't have to be grown up or able to believe anything before they are baptized. God's saving work that happens through baptism happens regardless of what we are able to believe or not. It's all a gift.

It makes complete sense when you think about it. When my children were born, I didn't think to myself, "now when Owen and Jesse can accept me as their mother and start doing the things I tell them to do, then I'm going to love them unconditionally and forgive them for the bad things they do and give them the gift of being their parent." Of course not. From the moment I heard their cries, from the moment I felt them move, from the moment they were even a possibility Chad and I whispered to each other, I loved them and knew I would give them everything I ever could. That is what a parent does. My love is not based on what they will do for me now or someday. It wouldn't be love if I felt that way. If we are made in God's image, then is it so strange to think that God would do the same for us? God gifts us with love and mercy and kindness. God does not wait for us to deserve it or ask for it.

Reformation Sunday is not a day we celebrate Lutherans. What is remarkable is not Lutheranism or Martin Luther or any of us; it is what God has done and continues to do.

For by works of the law no human being will be justified in his sight, since through the law comes knowledge of sin. But now the righteousness of

God has been manifested apart from the law, although the Law and the Prophets bear witness to it — the righteousness of God through faith in Jesus Christ for all who believe. For there is no distinction: for all have sinned and fall short of the glory of God, and are justified by his grace as a gift, through the redemption that is in Christ Jesus. — Romans 3:20-24

Prayer: Dear God, thank you for your grace upon grace. In Jesus name, I pray. Amen.

Reflect: If you belong to a denomination, what made you choose it? How much of your decision was based on theology? What were other factors that went into your decision?

Aspelund Lutheran Church
Flom, Minnesota

A Letter to my Sons

(This was from a sermon I preached right after the 2017 election)

My Dear Boys,

Your mom is a pastor. You have known this your whole lives. From the time you were only days old, you have come with me to visit people in nursing homes, hospitals, houses, and places of work. You have been with me, and you have bowed your little heads and prayed with us. It has been my greatest joy to share that with you and to see you come to know and love Jesus.

So, on a week like this, when there's been elections and shock and hurt and protests and winners and losers and those who are excited and those just plain terrified, I want to point your eyes away from the media, away from the divisiveness and ask you to focus the words of Saint Paul, *"whatever is true, whatever is noble, whatever is right, whatever is pure, whatever is lovely, whatever is admirable, excellent or praiseworthy"*. *(Philippians 4:8)* I need to remind you who you are as children of God, not just of your dad and me.

First, there's this: you remember a couple of years ago, that lady at the nursing home in Texas who frightened you one night? We were there visiting our congregation member, Estella, in those hard weeks right before she died and you two decided to wait for me on the big, soft chairs in the lobby while I went down the hall and prayed with Estella? One of the residents wheeled up to you as you were sitting there and told you to leave. She was confused and convinced you didn't belong there, and she yelled at you. You cried and you didn't understand why she was yelling at you, but you grabbed each other and came to find me in Estella's room. I could see how sad you were; your whole lives you had only known older folks to be kind to you, and suddenly this happened. We talked about how sometimes people get confused, especially after dark. Or maybe she had just had a terrible day and was upset about something else but took it out on you. We talked about how it didn't do any good to be angry about it; we just needed to respond with kindness and gentleness.

My dear boys, kindness is key. It always is. We don't know the battles others are fighting. We don't know half the demons that follow others around or the sadness that has bitten at their hearts. Whenever possible, be kind. Our Christian faith instructs us in this, *"Be ye kind one unto another, tenderhearted, forgiving one another, even as God for Christ's sake has forgiven you."* (Ephesians 4:32) And Jesus' words in Luke, *"If someone slaps you on one cheek, offer the other cheek also. If someone demands your coat, offer your shirt also."* (Luke 6:29) Kindness, mercy, grace, and forgiveness, are words that we hold close, cherish, and center ourselves around as people who believe in Jesus.

But, my dear boys, hear this: being kind is different than being complacent, complicit, a doormat, or even nice. Jesus himself, when he turned over the tables of the moneychangers in the temple, taught us to stand up for what is right. Jesus was always, on the side of the oppressed and spent time with those who lived on the margins – the poor, the outsiders, the refugees, those who had messed up big time, those with bad reputations. Jesus was all about finding ways to make room for everyone. He had no patience for leaving anyone behind or creating walls of division. Do you remember the Bible story where there was a group of people who were angry at a woman who had sinned, they thought she should die, but Jesus said, *"Okay, then, whoever among you has never sinned gets to be the first to throw a stone."* (John 8:1-7) And of course, no one could say they had never sinned. He pointed out that we are all sinners, all of us need forgiveness, we can't judge each other.

My boys, when I see you do something kind, my heart couldn't be more full. But I'll always pray, too, that when the time comes to call someone out who is being mean to or speaking badly about anyone because of their race, gender, political affiliation, sexual orientation, or for any reason, that you will have the strength to do that. Turn some tables over like Jesus did. Never be okay with injustice. Always speak up for those who are being bullied, no matter what age you are, or they are because this is the way of Jesus.

But even more than that, take it one more step. Don't just react to injustice, but work first to promote peace. How does this look? Well, every day it looks different, and for each person it looks different. Find ways to build community. Look for opportunities to build bridges. Jesus crossed boundaries and social barriers to share a message of love and peace, radical inclusivity, grace for all - and so as Christians, that is our goal, too. I promise, my dear boys, to keep looking for ways to do that, and you must, too. Because this is the way of Jesus.

Let's see, what else? There's so much. This task of living as Jesus' people is the most important thing you will do, but there is something that will help you: pray. Pray every day. Pray for those you like and especially for those you don't like.

Jesus said, *"Love your enemies and pray for those who persecute you."* *(Matthew 5:43-48)* And so we do. We pray for others, partly for them, but it helps us, too. Prayer can soften our hearts and ease our bitterness. It makes us better. We pray for our leaders and work hard speak respectfully of them, whether they were the one who received our vote or not. This, too, is the way of Jesus. We can work for change and disagree without slipping into speech that is beneath us. Be clear, be smart, be faithful, live passionately, but also watch your words because they always say more about you than they say about anyone else.

I remember like yesterday those June days when you were born. I held you close, looked at your little faces, and then I looked out at the Colorado mountains in the distance and I wondered what life would hold for you. So much was unknown. I was scared of becoming a mom, worried I would mess it up big time, worried I wouldn't have the kind of love and tenacity a parent needs to have. But then, we did what parents do, we gathered you up and took you home, trusting God would bring us through the journey of parenthood one day at a time. And God is faithful.

One day at a time, my dear boys. Trust God is with you. Be kind. Work for justice. Live peace. Pray. Follow Jesus.

I love you to the moon,

Mom

²⁹ Watch the way you talk. Let nothing foul or dirty come out of your mouth. Say only what helps, each word a gift.

³¹⁻³² Make a clean break with all cutting, backbiting, profane talk. Be gentle with one another, sensitive. Forgive one another as quickly and thoroughly as God in Christ forgave you. — Ephesians 4:29, 31-32

Prayer: Dear God, help me to teach the children in my life to follow your wisdom and guidance. Let me be a good example. In Jesus' name, I pray. Amen.

Reflect: If you had to sum up in a few sentences some wisdom for the generations that follow you, what would you say?

**My sons in front of Our Savior's Lutheran Church at Norse
Clifton, Texas**

Recluse

I woke up with a mild feeling of dread. The last thing I wanted to do was go back to work or be around people. The past few days I had spent reading and writing. Every few months I do this because I usually have piles of books I need to catch up on and I never seem to make enough time to write, so these days are necessary for me to stay connected to these essential tasks.

When I am coming out of a particularly busy week, it takes a couple of days for my mind to slow down and get into the groove of reading and writing and solitude, but once I am in that groove, it takes a great deal of effort to emerge back into civilization. When I left the house on Wednesday for an appointment, I realized I hadn't gone anywhere since Sunday except on a few lonesome walks in the neighboring fields. I also hadn't showered or brushed my hair. I can slip into hermit mode easily and could stay there indefinitely.

I come by it honestly. My dad was a full-fledged recluse. Many of my elementary-school classmates thought I didn't have a father because they never saw him, and unless they were in my house or the doctor's office, why would they? Those were the only places he spent his time.

I was still an infant and my brother only four when dad's health declined to the point he was unable to continue working as a pastor. We left the Twin Cities and moved to a tiny farmhouse outside Henning, Minnesota. Mom took care of my brother and me. Dad wrote. He fashioned a small office in a back room of the house where he retreated to scribble in his notebooks and read.

I believe he fancied our move to the country would be a new start for us. We raised chickens and had a big garden. On Sundays, he and mom taught us Sunday School at home. He knew the church in town could not teach us better than he could. On summer evenings, we played kickball in the backyard and during the winter, we went sledding down the big hill in the woods.

At first, Dad still did some supply preaching at area churches on Sundays, but he stopped that soon after we moved to the farmhouse. Dealing with people was too exhausting for him and bit by bit he began to delete himself from the world. He didn't run errands. He stopped working at all. He didn't have friends. He didn't visit his mother or brothers who lived five miles away. He never set foot in our school in the years Andrew and I were growing up. Eventually, he also stopped feeding the chickens and working in the garden. He finally wearily sent us to the church in town for Sunday School and confirmation class, and if we ever wanted to play kickball or go sledding, it was mom who went with us.

Our family narrative became "Dad doesn't feel good." "Dad is too sick" to come to this or that. "Dad is having a bad day," and so that's why he never leaves the house. He was suffering and he was the victim. The rest of us learned to live around that. We learned to never expect anything from him.

How infinitely small his world became. Perhaps it is no surprise he was angry much of the time – so angry that it seemed to push him over the edge to have to deal with any of us. His temper boiled and erupted into fits of yelling, hurling repetitive, paranoid, nonsensical phrases over and over until he would collapse into sleep on the scratchy brown living room couch. Finally, it wasn't enough to just isolate himself to our property or our house; he retreated to his bedroom where he laid in the dark quiet for years.

And I was glad when he finally did. It was so much easier when he stayed in that room because when he came out his anger and sadness filled me.

My dad had physical health issues, but it was the emotional and mental issues – the way he isolated himself - that took away his life. The isolation was the perfect nourishment for the depression that hid him away from us and everyone.

I've spent much of my adult life trying to make sense of my dad's life. While he and I were very different in some ways, it wouldn't be much of a leap to say that I appear to be living parts of his life. He was a pastor; I am a pastor. He loved living in the country; I love living in the country. He enjoyed writing and tended to that practice daily, praying it would be meaningful to someone else. So do I. His writing was his way of praying, telling himself and God about his life, worries, dreams, despair. Me, too.

There are two stories I tell over and over, and they are both stories of the loss of my parents. Although my parents died only a year apart, I lost one so much earlier than the other. Mom was 77 when she took her last breath, and we stopped being able to create new, loving memories with her. With Dad, it was about forty years before that when he stopped participating in life – his, mine, anyone's.

I grieve my mom's death, but I also grieve I lost my dad so long before he took his last breath. His physical death on a January day in 2010 was powerfully anticlimactic as he hadn't lived in so very long.

I want to live. I don't want anything to die in me while my heart is still beating.

Yes, I love my reading and writing days when I cloister myself away and talk to hardly anyone, but I know I must be with my community, too. I need them. I need their energy, ambition, love, and conflict because I have seen the alternative and it is empty. God didn't create us to exist only in our thoughts and comfortable, safe surroundings. Too much space, too much quiet, too much time alone – it seduces, but left unchecked, it kills. At least it kills me. I choose to be influenced by others – friends and acquaintances, to have their ideas rub up against mine and see what kind of fires ignite.

Not long ago, I was having a hard day. I was tired and hungry and grieving for a friend who had just lost her dad. On the drive back from the memorial service, I decided to pick up a pack of cigarettes. I quit long ago, but every few years I break down and buy a pack. I savor that pack over the next week until it is gone and then go back to my non-smoking life.

I thought about isolation that week because I didn't want anyone to know I was smoking, so I had to do it in secret. I made up reasons I could be alone so I could have a smoke: go for a drive, go for a walk, stay up after everyone went to bed, get up before everyone else, it was exhausting just trying to make room for those cigarettes in my life. Then, I also had to make sure I had breath mints and air freshener spray, and I was washing my hands constantly to try to keep the cigarette stench off of me. Alone, alone, alone. I craved that time alone like I craved the next smoke, but neither the time alone nor the nicotine fixed anything. I was not changed in a better way for having had that solitude or the smoke. I just felt increasingly isolated and morose.

What did help? What did bring ease and energy back again? Throwing away the few remaining cigarettes in the pack, putting on a nicotine patch and participating in life again. Laughing with my kids. Having coffee with a friend. Sitting down to talk to my husband. Singing hymns at the bar with my rowdy congregation.

We were created to be in community.

If you need to talk, I'm here.

If you know of someone who is lonesome, please give them a call.

24 And let us consider how to provoke one another to love and good deeds, 25 not neglecting to meet together, as is the habit of some, but encouraging one another, and all the more as you see the Day approaching. - Hebrews 10:24-25 (NRSV)

Prayer: Dear God, thank you for my community. Help me to love and serve them, laugh and cry with them, and share life day by day. Amen.

Reflect: What do you enjoy about being alone? What do you enjoy about being with others? Are you needing more time alone or more time in community than you are currently getting?

Lake Park Lutheran Church
Lake Park, Minnesota
(Layered with photo of tall grasses)

All Saints

All Saints Sunday is celebrated in the Lutheran church on the closest Sunday on or after All Saints Day, November 1st. It is a day to remember all the Saints, known and unknown. November 2nd is All Souls day, a day to remember those who have died.

Christian celebration of All Saints' Day and All Souls' Day stems from a belief that there is a powerful spiritual bond between those in heaven and those still on earth. In many congregations, the names of members of the congregation who have died in the last year are lifted up, and candles are lighted in memory of loved ones.

It's important to take time for remembering in ways such as this, to set aside to honor those relationships God gave us, those people we loved, even though we can't see or talk to them in the same way anymore. Our need for remembering doesn't end when the last breath is taken or when the memorial service is over or when the ashes are scattered. Grief goes on and our need to remember goes on. All Saints Sunday is a beautiful time set aside to do that.

Grieving is necessary, and there is no right or wrong way to do it. Some need to cry and wallow, some need to stay busy and distracted, some find meaning in creating a legacy in memory of their loved ones. Friends of mine whose son died established a scholarship in memory of their son. Their grief continues, but they are comforted that their son's name accompanies this scholarship which continues to help other young people.

There are countless ways to honor our significant relationships even after death. I recall the story of a man who traveled 600 miles, from North Carolina to Chicago, to listen to the last World Series game at his father's graveside. His father had been a lifelong Cubs fan and would always listen to games with his sons. They promised each other that when the Cubs won the World Series, no matter when, they would listen to the game together.

Any of us who have lost someone with whom we still had unfinished business, unfinished activities we wanted to do together, understand this. So often we look for ways to still feel connected to those who have died. We remember them when it's time to bake the Christmas cookies, when we go out to eat at the place where we used to meet and talk, when the birthday or anniversary comes and goes.

At the school my children attend, every year they celebrate a "Grandparents Day" when grandparents are invited to come to the school for special activities. Since my kids don't have any grandparents still alive, we invite their aunt and uncle who live nearby to come, but one year both my boys said they "didn't feel good" the morning of Grandparents Day. Neither of my kids is prone to "crying wolf" so I listened to them and let them stay home. However, when I came home from the office at noon, they were running around the house and obviously feeling physically fine. So, I took them out to lunch, and we had our own "Grandparents' Day." I made a quiz for them of twenty questions about their grandparents. Which grandparent loved Almond Joy candy bars? Which grandparent had the middle name "Cecil?" What did Grandma Dottie do for a living? They loved the questions and kept asking for more and we spent over an hour in the Chinese Restaurant in the strip mall talking about beloved members of our family whom my boys barely got to meet, yet we love them dearly and forever. While the purpose was to help my boys know and remember things about their grandparents, the process was therapeutic for me, too.

As we support one another through the losses that inevitably come with life, give one another opportunities to still speak about loved ones they have lost. Perhaps one of our prayers on All Saints Sunday could be that God helps all of us to remember to be mindful of each other and how we can gently accompany each other through the terrain of loss.

But there's more. On All Saints Sunday, we remember that while the pain of grief and separation is real, what is also real is that we are connected to one another for keeps. In churches like the one I serve, the old

Scandinavian altar rails tell a story way beyond architecture. The current congregation gathers around the visible half circle altar rail, while the circle is completed beyond time and space by those who have already died. The wholeness of that transcendent circle of all the saints makes a beautiful and powerful statement about the faith we profess and the hope to which we cling. We gather for worship in communion with all the saints throughout time, beyond space.

We are the communion of saints: You, me, your grandparents, Saint Augustine, Mother Teresa, Oscar Romero and a whole host of others – a motley crew of saints all of us. Old and young, dead and alive, short and tall, immigrant and native, democrat and republican and everything in-between, known to God by our best and truest name: Children of God.

This year at my church on All Saints, I gave slips of paper to everyone as they came in to worship and asked that they write the names of loved ones who have died on those slips of paper. Then, when they came up for communion, there were three glass vases inside the altar rail where they placed the names. We shared in communion and remembered that every time we gather there, those departed ones are also there.

That's a comforting thought to me – to think of mom in her brown polyester polka-dot dress and grandma with her ever-present tissues tucked up her sleeve or down the front of her dress, my dad with his cane and shriveled hands, my friend Candy with her pile of brown curls and a lit menthol cigarette – all of them still here with me, our heads bowed, thanking God for love, family, friendship, and so many mystical blessings that go way beyond time and space.

"Then I saw a new heaven and a new earth; for the first heaven and the first earth had passed away, and the sea was no more. And I saw the holy city, the new Jerusalem, coming down out of heaven from God, prepared as a bride adorned for her husband. And I heard a loud voice from the throne saying, "See, the home of God is among mortals. He will dwell with them as their God; they will be his peoples, and God himself will be with them; he will wipe every tear from their eyes. Death will be no more; mourning and crying and pain will be no more, for the first things have passed away." And the one who was seated on the throne said, "See, I am

making all things new." Also he said, "Write this, for these words are trustworthy and true." Then he said to me, "It is done! I am the Alpha and the Omega, the beginning and the end.- Revelation 21:1-6a

Prayer: Dear God, how I miss my loved ones who have died. Help me trust in your promises to them and to all of us. In Jesus' name, I pray. Amen.

Reflect: If right now you could have a conversation with any loved one who has died, who would it be? Why?

**Saint Peter's Lutheran Church
Audubon, Minnesota**

Saint Peter's Lutheran Church
Audubon, Minnesota

<u>All That We Let In</u>

Winter started early this year. Some years we can squeeze in some warmish days even in November, but not this year. By the end of October, snow began to slip down from the sky now and then, and by the time November started, it wasn't melting away between snowfalls. Today as I look out the church window, the field is covered with snow, and only a few tall clumps of overturned soil are visible. The sky is gray, the trees are a darker gray, the snow is white. Gray and white are the colors of this day.

A friend of mine who has always lived in Minnesota was wondering in a Facebook post why in the world he still lives here. His tone was weary, and any of us who live here can understand it. Living here takes a certain amount of tenacity. One has to be able to find the good in this long, cold season it and that is hard for those who don't like ice fishing, snowmobiling, skiing, sledding, etc. Personally, I'm not a fan of any of those things either but this year my younger son and I have committed to try snowshoeing. Maybe that will be our ticket to getting outside in the snow a bit more.

This is only my third winter back in Minnesota. I was away for 16 years: western New York (where the winters are worse than here), Colorado (where winters were about perfect – snow but also a lot of sunshine), and Texas (where it could easily be in the 80's on Christmas Day).

After five years in Texas, I was surprised I got to a point where I longed for a good blizzard. I didn't think it could be possible, but I eventually missed winter. I missed the great diversity of seasons that Minnesota has in abundance: bundling up and heading outside when snow is falling in fat, wet snowflakes; the first Spring days when the sun is just beginning to gather her strength again and people eagerly strip off the long layers to soak in as much Vitamin D as possible; summer days by the lakeshore when everyone is outside and lingering in conversation; the onset of crisp

Autumn and the leaves so colorful it takes your breath away. It's all these times and seasons and the moments in-between that make Minnesota fine by me. Each of these seasons stir memories because they are the same seasons I shared with my parents and friends when I was growing up. People who grew up other places don't understand it the way we do — how the snow can squeak and the air sounds tinny when it gets cold enough; how your heart aches to watch a perfect summer day come to an end because you know how precious those days are; how there is no smell as sweet and good as peonies and lilacs on a May morning; and the immensely bittersweet days of an unseasonably warm spell in October. I wanted my kids to understand this language, the difficulty and beauty of living in a place like this.

I'm committed to taking these winter days one at a time. They can't be rushed. We bake cookies and bread, I spend more time writing, I remind myself that Spring will come but now is the time to be in winter, I give thanks for my warm home and that I have a commute of 200 paces up to the church. I keep an eye on the weather and try to be out and about when it looks like the roads will be dry.

Wherever you go, there you are. There is so much to love about each place.

In Colorado, I climbed mountains on my day off. The sky was brilliantly blue most days, and it was hardly ever below zero degrees. The spirit of the people there was so free and I felt at home there. Most everyone I knew had transplanted there from somewhere else. It was easy to find a community in a place where everyone was searching for community.

There is no place like Texas where the bluebonnets and Indian paintbrush and all the wildflowers of the Spring were indescribably gorgeous. I could go running outside any day of the year and it was never too cold. In the summer, I just had to wait until the sun went down and the temperature was tamed a bit. There is no other place I have lived that was so wild, proud, and different from where I grew up.

Western New York was green, and the air was thick like soup in the summertime. I drove up to Toronto all the time, and I smoked one million cigarettes. They were hearty people who knew how to drive in extreme winter. They had a biting sense of humor I didn't understand.

I have called all these places home, and I was glad to do it while I did. I'm so grateful for all that came to my life because of those places and the people I met there. And it is good to call this winter place home again.

What do you love about the places you have called 'home'?

Lord, you have been our dwelling place for all generations. -Psalm 90:1

Prayer: Dear God, wherever we go, there You are. Thank you for this gorgeous world and all there is to see. Thank you for the joy of travel and the beauty of home. In Jesus' name, we pray. Amen.

Reflect: Why do you live where you live? Think about each place you have lived - what was a blessing God revealed to you there?

The former building of Good Shepherd Lutheran Church
Henning, Minnesota

Leave the Light On

The wind is whirling snow past the gravestones and clawing at the front doors of the church. Every now and then, the building creaks, but my office is warm.

It is the brief lull between Reformation Sunday and All Saints Sunday. My mother died during this lull in 2011. I left our church's Fall festival that Reformation Sunday to go to the hospital to see her. By that night I knew she was dying. She was so weary, so frail. I stayed as close to her bedside as I could while gracious friends helped to care for our little boys.

In the brief moments when she was awake, she was no longer speaking to me, but to loved ones beyond time and space. Connected to a million tubes, her skin paper-thin, after months of illness, she inexplicably began to smile and softly laugh as you do when thinking of old friends. When I asked her what she was saying, to be let in on the conversation, she looked dismayed. Her sights were no longer set on me, on this realm. She was looking ahead, looking forward, already gone in so many ways. Her body just had to catch up.

It was a Tuesday night when she died.

It was an early Wednesday morning when she died.

It was All Saints Day.

It was All Souls Day.

It was November 1.

It was November 2.

All of this is true to me because when I fell asleep on the hospital couch in her room on All Saints day, mom was still breathing. When I woke up on All Souls Day, I could no longer hear her breathing in the darkness, and I knew she was gone. I waited a few minutes before I went to turn on the light because I knew as soon as I saw her it would be real.

Finally, after minutes that felt like years, I got up and moved toward the light switch. I turned on the light and looked toward the bed. Sure enough. Her life had slipped away while I slept. Just like that.

I sat next to her as the nurses came in and out with their questions. I wanted to look at her dear face, but I kept focusing on her arms, her hands. I thought about all those hands had held: me and my brother when we were babies, they cared for my dad all the years he was sick, they typed up church bulletins and newsletters, they washed countless loads of laundry and dishes, baked bread and birthday cakes, they held the handkerchief she carried around for when tears snuck up on her, they had held a whole lifetime, and now their work was done.

In slow-motion, I made the calls I needed to make. It was still the middle of the night, and the world was sleeping. I left messages for my husband, my brother. With no one in my family awake to talk to me at that bleak hour, the funeral director from Minnesota who had handled my father's funeral the year before was a warm and welcome voice. His northern accent was comforting as I sat there in that Texas hospital. He sounded like home.

The room was needed for patients who were still alive, and so it was time to go. I touched her cool hand one more time and then walked out to my car. The city of Waco was hushed in that early morning hour, and it was raining slightly. I noted to myself how the world felt so different now, and of course, it was. It was now a world that no longer had my mother's smile, voice, and wisdom in it. A world so sorely lacking for having lost those precious things.

And now, somehow nearly seven years have passed since that night/morning. I've gone to sleep and woken up thousands of times in a world where my mom isn't. My boys hardly remember her, but they know well my stories of her. They know that their mom loved her mom and there's a well of sadness that still springs up out of me sometimes, and that's okay. My shiny stone of grief I carry around is precious to me because it's one of the ways I hold on to her.

But it is just one of the ways. There are so many other ways I remember her, too, and as the years pass, I want to be better at remembering her differently.

I want to remember her with laughter because she loved to laugh. Her laugh was like silver bells over the snow: light and sweet. She laughed easily and often.

I want to remember her by being a good friend because she treasured her friends. In the challenges and changes of life, her friends were her anchor and joy. She made time for them, and they were fiercely devoted to each other.

I want to remember her by being a great mom. She loved being a mother, and she excelled at building a home. Not necessarily the tasks of being a housewife – she hated cleaning, she wasn't a remarkable cook, she cared little about decorating, but she knew how to make a home. She made time for us kids, giving us herself, always.

I want to remember her by welcoming my years. Mom was not vain. She was present in whatever age she was at. She didn't have time for nonsense. She lived the life God gave her, neither rushing the years nor wishing for the past to return.

I want to remember her by being me. That's all she ever wanted for me. She gave me roots and then she gave me wings, and she would be so disappointed if I didn't fly and be the weird, soft-spoken, bookish, restless person God made me to be.

It does me no good to build a monument of pain in memory of her. I didn't mean to do that, but in many ways, I have. I'll always think of her, miss her, share stories about her, but I don't want the narrative I tell about my mom for the rest of my days to be full of sadness when her life was not that way. She was joy and laughter and friendship. She was peace and gentleness, a "yes" to love and goodness.

At our house in the country where I grew up, we had a yard light out by the garage. If my brother or I were out past dark, mom would turn on that yard light so that we would have a light to welcome us home. It was such a small thing, but so lovely to turn the corner onto our lonesome gravel road and see that light in the distance. It was mom saying, "I'm thinking of you. Be safe! Come home soon. Welcome back." She continued to do that long after we had moved away from home. If we were coming for a visit and arrived after dark, the light would be on.

Perhaps the rest of my days, my task is to remember to leave the light on for other people. For my children, by loving them the best I can, giving them the best of my time, and a warm and welcoming place to call home. For my congregation, by pointing them toward Jesus, caring for them, and helping our church be a place of grace. For my friends, by being supportive and listening, and sharing of myself. For strangers, by offering help, a smile, hospitality.

Leave the light on. This is how I choose to remember my mom for the rest of my days to come.

14-16 *"Here's another way to put it: You're here to be light, bringing out the God-colors in the world. God is not a secret to be kept. We're going public with this, as public as a city on a hill. If I make you light-bearers, you don't think I'm going to hide you under a bucket, do you? I'm putting you on a light stand. Now that I've put you there on a hilltop, on a light stand— shine! Keep open house; be generous with your lives. By opening up to others, you'll prompt people to open up with God, this generous Father in heaven. - Matthew 5:16 The Message (MSG)*

Prayer: Dear God, lead me by Your light and help share Your light. In Jesus' name, I pray. Amen.

Reflect: What is one way you can "leave the light on" for someone today?

Gran Lutheran Church
Hawley, Minnesota

Tunbridge Lutheran Church
Pierce County, North Dakota

Mom and me – 2001

Made in the USA
San Bernardino, CA
21 April 2018